THE NO-FUSS
COLLEGE
COOKBOOK

FUEL YOUR BRAIN WITH 150+ EASY, WHOLESOME, AND AFFORDABLE RECIPES FOR BUSY STUDENTS

LYDIA MERRILL

THE NO-FUSS
COLLEGE
COOKBOOK

FUEL YOUR BRAIN WITH DELICIOUS, EASY, AND HEALTHY
AFFORDABLE MEALS FOR THE BUSY STUDENTS

LYDIA MERRILL

Published by Aries Publishing Ltd (www.bonusliber.com)
Contact: admin@bonusliber.com
Editors: James Peters, Melissa Fields

First Edition: May 2023

INDICE

"Knowledge is the food of the soul, and you must not starve it. So is food the knowledge of the body, and you must not let it hunger. Feed both, for a balanced life."

INTRODUCTION

Hey there, and welcome to "The No-Fuss Student's Cookbook!"

So, you're a college student, huh? Well, you know the drill – it's all about balancing academics, social life, and personal growth. And guess what? Eating right is a big part of staying on top of your game during these wild and transformative years. Trust me; I've been there. With all your responsibilities, finding the time and money to eat healthily can feel like a Herculean task. But hey, that's where this cookbook comes in to save the day.I'm the author of this book, and I've got my fair share of experience with college students' struggles with eating well. I remember my college days – juggling classes, part-time jobs, and extracurriculars while trying to stay healthy. It was quite a challenge! But you know what? I learned that you could cook up some delicious and nutritious meals without breaking the bank or spending all day in the kitchen.

Oh, I've got to tell you this one story from my college days that still brings a smile to my face. You see, my cooking skills actually made me quite popular on campus – who would've thought? It all started when I began hosting casual dinner parties for my friends in my tiny dorm room. I'd whip up some of my favorite recipes from scratch, and let me tell you, the aromas wafting through the halls were enough to draw a crowd!

Word spread quickly; before I knew it, I had people knocking on my door, asking if they could join in on the fun. My dorm room became the go-to spot for mouthwatering meals and good company, and it wasn't long before I earned a reputation as the "dorm room chef." It was such an incredible experience to see how my cooking brought people together, sparking lively conversations and fostering long-lasting connections and friendships.

This just goes to show how amazingly powerful food can be in creating connections and memories. My cooking skills not only helped me stay healthy during college but also opened up a whole new world of social opportunities. As you explore the recipes in this cookbook and develop your cooking skills, I hope you will also create unforgettable moments, forge new friendships, and maybe even become the "dorm room chef" everyone raves about!

This realization led me down the path of becoming a Certified Dietician and Nutritionist. Now that I've got years of professional experience, I'm super excited to share my knowledge and love for healthy cooking with you. This book is your ultimate guide to navigating the world of cooking, packed with simple, tasty, and budget-friendly recipes tailored just for busy college students like you.

I know your time is precious, so we've handpicked easy-peasy recipes that require minimal equipment and ingredients and still taste amazing. With a wide range of cuisines, dietary preferences, and skill levels, we've got you covered – from breakfast to dinner, snacks, and even desserts. There's something for everyone, whether you're a newbie in the kitchen or a seasoned home chef.

But wait, there's more! We've got advice on meal planning, grocery shopping, and organizing your kitchen like a pro. Throughout the book, you'll find handy tips and tricks to make your cooking experience more fun and efficient.

As you dive into this culinary adventure, remember that cooking is more than just a life skill – it's a way to stay healthy, get creative, and connect with others. Sharing a meal with friends, family or even just treating yourself can be incredibly rewarding. I truly hope "The No-Fuss Student's Cookbook" becomes your go-to resource for delicious, wholesome meals throughout your college life and beyond.

So, what are you waiting for? Let's get cooking and fuel your brain with these easy, wholesome, affordable recipes for busy students like you. Happy cooking, and bon appétit!

HEALTHY EATING AND STUDYING

Eating well is crucial for keeping you feeling great, especially while you're in college. As a college student, you are navigating a transformative life period characterized by increased independence, academic challenges, and personal growth. A balanced diet keeps you physically healthy and supports your cognitive function and emotional well-being, which are essential for your success and happiness during this critical phase.

Here are a few reasons why healthy eating is essential for college students:

- Improved cognitive function: A nutritious diet can have a significant impact on your cognitive abilities, including memory, focus, and concentration. Brain-boosting meals, including whole grains, lean protein, fruits, veggies, and healthy fats, can help increase your academic performance and overall productivity.

- Increased energy: A balanced diet provides the necessary fuel to power through your busy schedule, including attending classes, studying, engaging in extracurricular activities, and maintaining a social life. By making healthier food choices, you'll be able to sustain your energy levels throughout the day and avoid the crashes associated with unhealthy, processed foods.

- Enhanced immune system: College life exposes you to various stressors, such as academic pressure, lack of sleep, and communal living. These factors can weaken your immune system, making you more susceptible to illnesses. A balanced and nutritious diet rich in vitamins and minerals can help maintain the wellness and power of your immune system.

- Better mental health: Nowadays, everybody knows that diet and mental health are closely linked. A balanced diet, rich in whole foods and essential nutrients, can help alleviate stress, anxiety, and depression. By making healthier food choices, you'll be better equipped to manage your emotions and maintain a positive outlook on life.

- Weight management: Many college students struggle with weight gain due to stress, lack of exercise, and unhealthy eating habits. Eating a balanced diet and regular physical activity can help you maintain a healthy weight and prevent obesity-related health issues.

- Long-term health benefits: Developing healthy eating habits during college sets the foundation for lifelong wellness. By making nutritious food choices now, you're reducing your risk of developing chronic diseases, such as heart disease, diabetes, and certain types of cancer, later in life.

- Budget-friendly: Contrary to popular belief, healthy eating does not have to be extravagant. Meal planning, smart purchasing, and cooking at home can help you save money while eating healthy, scrumptious food.

THE BENEFITS OF COOKING ON YOUR OWN

Cooking on your own as a college student might initially seem daunting. However, the benefits of taking the time to learn and practice basic cooking skills far outweigh the challenges. With a little practice and creativity, you'll soon discover the joy of creating delicious, wholesome meals that fuel your body and mind.

Health Benefits

One of the most significant benefits of cooking on your own is the ability to control your meals' ingredients and portion sizes, leading to healthier eating habits, as you can choose fresh, nutrient-dense foods and avoid overly processed options. By learning to cook with whole, unprocessed ingredients, you can ensure your body gets the vitamins, minerals, and macronutrients it needs to function optimally, boosting your energy levels, cognitive function, and overall well-being.

Financial Savings

Eating out or relying on takeout and delivery can quickly add up, causing a strain on your limited student budget. By cooking at home, you can save a considerable amount of money. Shopping for groceries and planning meals beforehand allows you to take advantage of sales and bulk purchasing. Additionally, preparing large batches of food can result in leftovers, providing you with multiple meals for the price of one.

Developing Valuable Life Skills

Cooking is a valuable life skill that can benefit you long after your college years. As you learn to cook, you'll also develop better time management, organizational skills, and problem-solving abilities. You'll become more self-reliant and resourceful as you experiment with different recipes, ingredients, and cooking techniques. These skills will serve you well in various aspects of life, from professional to personal.

Social Opportunities and Bonding

Cooking on your own doesn't have to be a solitary activity. Sharing your culinary creations with others can develop bonds and foster companionship. Also, cooking with friends or roommates can be an enjoyable and intriguing social experience. Furthermore, hosting potlucks or dinner parties with classmates allows you to expand your social circle while enjoying a delicious, home-cooked meal.

Personalizing Your Food Preferences

By cooking for yourself, you can tailor your meals to your specific tastes and dietary needs. Whether you have allergies, follow a particular diet, or simply have strong food preferences, you can create dishes that cater to your unique requirements. This increases your enjoyment of your meals and ensures you meet your Nutritional needs.

Stress Relief and Creative Outlet

Cooking can serve as a therapeutic and creative outlet that provides a welcome break and a distraction from the strains of college life. Making your own dinner can be a peaceful and comforting activity that allows you to focus on the present moment and briefly forget about academic responsibilities. Moreover, experimenting with new recipes and techniques can foster a sense of accomplishment and boost your self-confidence.

TIPS FOR MEAL PLANNING AND GROCERY SHOPPING

Meal planning and grocery shopping that saves time and money are vital for college students who want to eat healthily without spending a fortune. Here are some useful tips to help you streamline your meal planning and grocery shopping experience.

1. Plan your meals: Before heading to the grocery store, plan your weekly meals. This will help you create a focused shopping list, reducing the time spent on wandering through aisles and making impulse purchases. It also helps prevent food waste by buying only what you need.

2. Create a master shopping list: Keep a running list of items you frequently use in your recipes. This will save time when creating your weekly shopping list and ensure you don't forget any essentials.

3. Shop with a list: Always go grocery shopping with a list in hand to avoid impulse purchases and ensure you get everything you need. Stick to your list and avoid wandering down aisles filled with tempting, unhealthy options.

4. Choose versatile ingredients: Opt for ingredients that can be used in different recipes throughout the week. For example, buying a rotisserie chicken can provide protein for several meals, such as sandwiches, salads, or pasta dishes.

5. Buy in bulk: When possible, purchase non-perishable items and frequently used ingredients in bulk. This can save money in the long term since bulk items are generally cheaper per unit. To keep bulk items fresh and prevent spoilage, store them carefully.

6. Opt for store brands: Store brands often offer the same quality as name-brand products at a lower cost. Don't be afraid to give them a try to save some money.

7. Take advantage of sales and coupons: Pay attention to weekly sales and use coupons to save on items you regularly purchase. Plan your meals around sale items, especially proteins and fresh produce, to maximize savings.

8. Embrace frozen and canned products: Frozen and canned fruits and vegetables can be more affordable and have a longer shelf life than fresh produce. They also retain much of their Nutritional values, making them a great option for students on a budget.

9. Shop the perimeter: Grocery stores are typically designed with fresh, whole foods around the perimeter and processed foods in the middle aisles. By shopping mainly around the perimeter, you'll naturally make healthier choices and save money by avoiding pre-packaged, processed items.

10. Cook in batches: Prepare larger quantities of food and freeze leftovers for future meals. This can save both time and money, as you'll have meals ready to go when you're short on time or low on funds.

11. Limit trips to the grocery store: Try to shop once a week or every other week, as this reduces the chances of making impulse purchases and helps you stick to your meal plan and budget.

12. Invest in food storage containers: Having a variety of reusable food storage containers makes storing leftovers and prepped ingredients easy, allowing you to keep organized and minimize food waste.

KITCHEN ESSENTIALS

Setting up your kitchen for the first time? No worries, I've got you covered. Here's a list of must-have kitchen items that will make the cooking experience more enjoyable and simple:

- Knives: Dude, you need a good set of knives! At the very least, grab a chef's, serrated, and paring knife. These three amigos will help you tackle most cutting tasks, from slicing bread to chopping veggies.

- Cutting board: Get yourself a sturdy, non-slip cutting board to protect your countertops and make food prep safer. Bonus points if it's dishwasher-safe for easy cleanup!

- Measuring cups and spoons: You have to measure stuff, right? Invest in a set of measuring cups and spoons for both dry and liquid ingredients.

- Mixing bowls: A set of mixing bowls in various sizes will make meal preparation and mixing so much easier. For added convenience, look for ones with non-slip bases and handles.

- Pots and pans: Grab a basic cookware set with a non-stick frying pan, a medium-sized saucepan with a lid, and a large pot for boiling pasta or making soups. Choose durable, easy-to-clean materials like stainless steel or anodized aluminum.

- Baking sheet: A rimmed baking sheet is just versatile and can be used for roasting veggies, baking cookies, or even cooking a sheet pan dinner.

- Colander or strainer: A colander is essential for draining pasta, washing fruits and veggies, and straining liquids from canned goods.

- Cooking utensils: Stock up on a spatula, slotted spoon, and tongs. These basic utensils will make cooking and serving all sorts of dishes easier.

- Can opener: You'll need a reliable can opener for those canned goods that'll inevitably end up in your pantry.

- Food storage containers: Get a variety of food storage containers in different sizes for storing leftovers, prepped ingredients, and pantry items. Go for airtight, leak-proof containers for maximum freshness and convenience.

- Microwave-safe dishes: Pick up some microwave-safe bowls and plates for reheating leftovers or cooking quick, microwaveable meals.

- Dish towels and pot holders: Keep a few dish towels and pot holders handy for drying dishes, wiping up spills, and handling hot pots and pans.

- Kitchen timer: You don't want to overcook or undercook your meals, right? A timer is essential. You can use your smartphone's built-in timer, but a dedicated kitchen timer can be super helpful too.

PANTRY STAPLES AND BASIC INGREDIENTS

Alright, folks! Let's talk about the backbone of your college kitchen: pantry staples and basic ingredients. Having these essentials in your kitchen will make whipping up delicious and nutritious meals a breeze. Plus, you'll save time and money by not having to run to the store for last-minute ingredients.

Here's a list of some pantry staples and basic ingredients that you'll want to have on hand:

- Grains and pasta: These provide the base for many meals and are super versatile. Some good options in your pantry include rice, quinoa, oats, and your favorite pasta shapes.

- Canned goods: Canned beans, vegetables, and fruits can be lifesavers on busy days. They have a long shelf life and are ready to use whenever needed.

- Cooking oils: A good quality cooking oil is essential for sautéing, frying, and baking. Olive oil, canola oil, or vegetable oil are all great options.

- Spices and seasonings: Salt, pepper, onion powder, garlic powder, and a handful of your favorite spices can go a long way toward making your food more flavorful.

- Baking essentials: Flour, sugar, baking powder, and baking soda are key ingredients for whipping up homemade baked goods.

Let me give you an example of how having these pantry staples can come in handy. Picture this: it's a weeknight, and you've just returned from a long day of classes, followed by a group project meeting. You're tired and hungry but don't want to spend money on takeout. Instead, you check your pantry and see that you have rice, canned black beans, canned corn, and some spices. You can quickly whip up a tasty and filling rice bowl topped with beans, corn, and a sprinkle of your favorite herbs with these ingredients. Thanks to your well-stocked pantry, you'll have a delicious meal that doesn't require much effort.

Keeping a range of basic ingredients on hand lets you come up with great meals without having to run to the store every time you want to cook. Furthermore, mixing these ingredients in novel ways allows you to experiment with new flavors and recipes, making your college cooking experience more enjoyable and less monotonous. So go ahead and stock up on these essentials, and you'll be well-prepared for any mealtime situation that comes your way!

UNDERSTANDING HERBS, SPICES, AND FLAVOR PROFILES

All right, let me tell you a little personal story. When I first started cooking in college, I was that person who thought salt and pepper were the only seasonings I'd ever need. Boy, was I wrong! One day, a friend invited me over for dinner, and I was absolutely blown away by the flavors in her dishes. When I asked her what her secret was, she simply said, "Herbs and spices." That's when I learned these magical ingredients truly had the power to transform even the most ordinary dish into something spectacular.

Herbs and spices are like the secret assets in your kitchen. They give depth, character, and complexity to your meals, elevating them from "just okay" to "OMG, this is amazing!" Plus, they're a fantastic way to explore new cuisines and experiment with different flavor profiles. So, let's dive into the wonderful world of herbs and spices and learn how to use them to your advantage!

- Fresh vs. Dried Herbs: Fresh herbs pack a punch with their vibrant flavors, while dried herbs tend to have a more concentrated taste. Both have their place in the kitchen but remember that dried herbs are typically more potent, so you'll need to adjust the quantity accordingly. A general rule of thumb is to use three times as many fresh herbs as dried herbs.

- Common Herbs: Some popular herbs you should consider keeping on hand include basil, cilantro, parsley, rosemary, thyme, and oregano. These versatile herbs can be used in various dishes, from pasta and soups to roasted veggies and grilled meats, making your meals more tasteful.

- Spice It Up: A well-stocked spice cabinet can make all the difference in your cooking. Ground cumin, paprika, chili powder, coriander, cinnamon, nutmeg, and turmeric are all must-have spices. These spices can be combined to create a wide range of flavors, so don't be afraid to experiment. It's time to get creative!

- Building Flavor Profiles: Understanding how to combine herbs and spices is key to creating flavorful dishes. To get started, get to know the typical flavor profiles of different cuisines. For example, Italian dishes often feature basil, oregano, and garlic, while Mexican cuisine relies heavily on cumin, chili powder, and cilantro. You'll be able to make authentic-tasting foods with ease if you understand these combos.

- Taste as You Go: The ideal way to learn about herbs, spices, and flavor profiles is to taste your food while you cook. This will allow you to experiment with different combinations and adjust the spices, allowing you to develop and refine your cooking skills.

Overall, don't be scared to venture beyond salt and pepper and embrace the incredible world of herbs and spices. These flavorful ingredients have the power to revolutionize your cooking and take your dishes to the next level. So get adventurous, and let your taste buds lead the way!

BREAKFAST - FUELING YOUR MORNINGS THE RIGHT WAY

Ah, breakfast. The meal we've all been told since we were toddlers is the most important one of the day. But let me tell you something, when I was a college student, I often found myself on the run, grabbing whatever was handy or skipping breakfast altogether. I know, not good, right?

As a dietician in my 40s, I can't emphasize enough how important a proper breakfast is to kickstart your day and prepare you for a productive one.

In this chapter, we'll delve into the magic of breakfast and show you that it doesn't have to be a chore. I've split these delicious breakfast recipes into two mouth-watering categories: Quick and Healthy Breakfast Ideas and Weekend Breakfast Treats. Believe me, there's something for everyone, whether you're rushing to a morning lecture or lounging around on a lazy Sunday.

Let me share a little anecdote from my college days with you. I used to live off of vending machine snacks and cold pizza for breakfast - I know, not the healthiest choices, right? It wasn't until I started exploring healthier options that I noticed a significant improvement in my energy levels and ability to concentrate in class. If only I had this cookbook back then!

Quick and Healthy Breakfast Ideas are designed for those hectic weekday mornings when time is not on your side. These recipes are easy to make, high in nutrients, and ideal for eating on the go. From overnight oats to yogurt parfaits, you'll find that these recipes will make your mornings a breeze while also fueling your body and mind for the day ahead.

Weekend Breakfast Treats, on the other hand, are your go-to recipes for those leisurely mornings when you can take a little extra time to treat yourself. You'll find indulgent yet well-balanced dishes like fluffy pancakes and delectable omelets. I guarantee your taste buds and body will thank you for these weekend goodies.

So, get ready, college students, because I am about to change the way you eat breakfast forever! Say goodbye to cold pizza and vending machine fare and hello to the energizing world of breakfast done right! With the following recipes, you'll see that you can indeed have it all - delicious, nutritious meals that fit seamlessly into your busy schedule.

PART I: QUICK AND HEALTHY BREAKFAST

OVERNIGHT BRAIN-BOOSTING OATS

 PREP TIME: 10 MINUTES   **SERVINGS: 2**   **CHILL TIME: 8 HOURS**

INGREDIENTS:

- 1 cup old-fashioned rolled oats
- 1 cup unsweetened almond milk (or milk of your choice)
- 1/2 cup plain Greek yogurt
- 1 tablespoon chia seeds
- 1 tablespoon honey (or maple syrup)
- 1/2 teaspoon vanilla extract
- 1/4 teaspoon ground cinnamon
- 1 medium apple, diced
- 1/4 cup chopped walnuts
- 1/4 cup dried cranberries or raisins

DIRECTIONS:

1. Combine the rolled oats, almond milk, Greek yogurt, chia seeds, honey, vanilla extract, and ground cinnamon in a medium-sized mixing bowl. Stir until well combined.
2. Add the diced apple, chopped walnuts, and dried cranberries or raisins to the oat mixture, and stir gently to incorporate.
3. Divide the mixture evenly between two mason jars or airtight containers, and secure the lids.
4. Place the containers in the refrigerator and let them chill overnight or for at least 8 hours.
5. When you're ready to enjoy your breakfast, stir the oats well and enjoy cold or warmed-up in the microwave for a nutritious start to your day.

Nutritional values: Calories: 385, Fat: 14g, Saturated Fat: 1.5g, Cholesterol: 0mg, Sodium: 65mg, Carbohydrates: 55g, Fiber: 9g, Sugars: 22g, Protein: 15g

GREEK YOGURT PARFAIT WITH GRANOLA AND BERRIES

 PREP TIME: 5 MINUTES   **SERVINGS: 1**

INGREDIENTS:

- 1 cup Greek yogurt (plain or vanilla)
- 1/2 cup mixed berries (such as strawberries, blueberries, raspberries, and blackberries)
- 1/3 cup granola (preferably low-sugar)
- 1 tbsp honey (optional)
- 1 tbsp chopped nuts (optional, such as almonds, walnuts, or pecans)

DIRECTIONS:

1. In a glass or bowl, layer 1/2 cup of Greek yogurt at the bottom.
2. Add 1/4 cup of mixed berries on top of the yogurt.
3. Sprinkle 1/2 of the granola (1/6 cup) over the berries.
4. Repeat the layers with the remaining yogurt, berries, and granola.
5. If desired, drizzle honey on top and sprinkle with chopped nuts for added crunch.
6. Grab a spoon and enjoy your delicious and nutritious parfait!

Nutritional values: Calories: 350 kcal, Protein: 20 g, Carbohydrates: 45 g, Sugars: 25 g, Fiber: 6 g, Fat: 12 g, Saturated Fat: 2 g, Unsaturated Fat: 10 g, Cholesterol: 10 mg, Sodium: 80 mg

VEGGIE-PACKED BREAKFAST BURRITO

 PREP TIME: 10 MINUTES   **SERVINGS: 1**

DIRECTIONS:

1. In a non-stick skillet, heat the olive oil or cooking spray over medium heat. Add the diced bell pepper, onion, and sauté until softened and slightly browned, about 3-4 minutes.
2. Whisk the eggs with a pinch of salt and pepper in a small bowl. Pour the beaten eggs into the skillet with the veggies, and let them sit for a moment before gently stirring to scramble.
3. Add the chopped spinach to the skillet and cook for an additional 1-2 minutes, until the eggs are fully cooked, and the spinach has wilted.
4. Warm the tortilla in the microwave for 10-15 seconds or in a separate skillet over low heat for about 30 seconds on each side.
5. Lay the warm tortilla on a plate, and spoon the egg and veggie mixture onto one side of the tortilla. Sprinkle the grated cheese on top of the egg mixture.
6. Fold the tortilla half over the filling, then roll it up from one end to form a burrito. If desired, serve with hot sauce or salsa on the side for an extra kick.
7. Enjoy your nutritious and tasty veggie-packed breakfast burrito!

INGREDIENTS:

- 1 whole-grain or whole-wheat tortilla (8-inch)
- 2 large eggs
- 1/4 cup diced bell pepper (any color)
- 1/4 cup diced onion
- 1/4 cup chopped spinach
- 1/4 cup grated cheese (such as cheddar or Monterey Jack)
- 1 tbsp olive oil or cooking spray
- Salt and pepper, to taste
- Optional: hot sauce or salsa for serving

Nutritional values: Calories: 450 kcal, Protein: 23 g, Carbohydrates: 35 g, Sugars: 4 g, Fiber: 5g, Fat: 25 g, Saturated Fat: 8 g, Unsaturated Fat: 17 g, Cholesterol: 380 mg, Sodium: 550 mg

ALMOND BUTTER AND BANANA RICE CAKE

 PREP TIME: 5 MINUTES   **SERVINGS: 1**

INGREDIENTS:

- 1 brown rice cake (unsalted)
- 2 tbsp almond butter (or any nut butter of your choice)
- 1 small banana, sliced
- 1 tsp chia seeds (optional)
- 1 tsp honey or maple syrup (optional)
- Dash of ground cinnamon (optional)

DIRECTIONS:

1. Spread the almond butter evenly on top of the rice cake.
2. Arrange the banana slices on top of the almond butter in a single layer.
3. If desired, sprinkle chia seeds over the banana slices for added texture and nutrition.
4. For a touch of sweetness, drizzle honey or maple syrup over the top, and add a dash of ground cinnamon for extra flavor if you like.
5. Enjoy your quick, delicious, healthy almond butter and banana rice cake!

Nutritional values: Calories: 330 kcal, Protein: 8 g, Carbohydrates: 42 g, Sugars: 19 g, Fiber: 6g, Fat: 16 g, Saturated Fat: 1.5 g, Unsaturated Fat: 14.5 g, Sodium: 50 mg

GREEN SMOOTHIE WITH SPINACH, AVOCADO, AND ALMOND MILK

 PREP TIME: 5 MINUTES    SERVINGS: 1

INGREDIENTS:

- 1 cup fresh spinach, packed
- 1/2 ripe avocado, peeled and pitted
- 1/2 banana, frozen
- 1 cup unsweetened almond milk
- 1 tbsp chia seeds or flaxseeds (optional)
- 1/2 cup ice cubes
- Optional sweetener: honey or maple syrup, to taste

Nutritional values: Calories: 200 kcal, Protein: 4 g, Carbohydrates: 21 g, Sugars: 9 g, Fiber: 8 g, Fat: 12 g, Saturated Fat: 1.5 g, Unsaturated Fat: 10.5 g, Sodium: 180 mg

DIRECTIONS:

1. In a blender, combine the spinach, avocado, frozen banana, and almond milk. If using chia seeds or flaxseeds, add them as well.
2. Blend on high speed until smooth and creamy. If the smoothie is too thick, add a little more almond milk to reach your desired consistency.
3. Add the ice cubes and blend again until well combined and chilled.
4. Taste the smoothie and, if desired, add honey or maple syrup to sweeten it to your liking. Blend once more to mix in the sweetener.
5. Pour the green smoothie into a glass and enjoy your refreshing, nutrient-packed breakfast!

CHIA SEED PUDDING WITH FRESH FRUIT

 PREP TIME:5 MINUTES (PLUS AT LEAST 2 HOURS OF CHILLING TIME)    SERVINGS: 1

INGREDIENTS:

- 1/4 cup chia seeds
- 1 cup unsweetened almond milk (or milk of your choice)
- 1/2 tsp vanilla extract
- 1 tbsp honey or maple syrup (optional)
- 1/2 cup fresh fruit (such as berries, mango, or kiwi), chopped
- Optional toppings: shredded coconut, chopped nuts, or granola

Nutritional values: Calories: 300 kcal, Protein: 10 g, Carbohydrates: 35 g, Sugars: 17 g, Fiber: 14 g, Fat: 14 g, Saturated Fat: 1.5 g, Unsaturated Fat: 12.5 g, Sodium: 180 mg

DIRECTIONS:

1. In a mason jar or airtight container, combine the chia seeds, almond milk, and vanilla extract. Stir well to combine, making sure the chia seeds are evenly distributed.
2. If desired, add honey or maple syrup to sweeten the mixture to your liking, and stir well to incorporate.
3. Seal the container with a lid or plastic wrap, and refrigerate for at least 2 hours or overnight for best results. The chia seeds will absorb the liquid and thicken into a pudding-like consistency.
4. Once the chia seed pudding has thickened, stir it well to break up any clumps.
5. Top the pudding with your choice of fresh fruit and any additional toppings, such as shredded coconut, chopped nuts, or granola.
6. Dig in and enjoy your delicious and healthy chia seed pudding with fresh fruit!

APPLE CINNAMON QUINOA BREAKFAST BOWL

 PREP TIME: 20 MINUTES   **SERVINGS: 1**

INGREDIENTS:

- 1/2 cup cooked quinoa (prepared according to package instructions)
- 1 small apple, cored and chopped
- 1/4 cup unsweetened almond milk (or milk of your choice)
- 1/2 tsp ground cinnamon
- 1/4 tsp ground nutmeg
- 1 tbsp honey or maple syrup (optional)
- Optional toppings: chopped nuts, dried fruit, or a dollop of Greek yogurt

Nutritional values: Calories: 280 kcal, Protein: 6 g, Carbohydrates: 50 g, Sugars: 20 g, Fiber: 6 g, Fat: 6 g, Saturated Fat: 0.5 g, Unsaturated Fat: 5.5 g, Sodium: 100 mg

DIRECTIONS:

1. In a small saucepan, combine the cooked quinoa, chopped apple, almond milk, cinnamon, and nutmeg. Stir well to combine.

2. Cook the quinoa mixture over medium-low heat for 5-7 minutes, stirring occasionally, until the apple is tender and the quinoa has absorbed most of the almond milk.

3. If desired, sweeten the quinoa mixture with honey or maple syrup, and stir well to incorporate.

4. Transfer the apple cinnamon quinoa to a bowl and let it cool slightly.

5. Top the quinoa breakfast bowl with your choice of optional toppings, such as chopped nuts, dried fruit, or a dollop of Greek yogurt.

6. Enjoy your warm, nutritious, and delicious apple cinnamon quinoa breakfast bowl!

PEANUT BUTTER AND JELLY PROTEIN SHAKE

 PREP TIME: 5 MINUTES   **SERVINGS: 1**

INGREDIENTS:

- 1 cup unsweetened almond milk (or milk of your choice)
- 1 scoop (about 30 g) of vanilla protein powder
- 1 tbsp natural peanut butter (or any nut butter of your choice)
- 1/4 cup frozen mixed berries
- 1/2 frozen banana
- 1/2 cup ice cubes
- Optional: honey or maple syrup, to taste

DIRECTIONS:

1. In a blender, combine the almond milk, vanilla protein powder, peanut butter, frozen mixed berries, and frozen banana.

2. Blend on high speed until smooth and creamy. If the shake is too thick, add a little more almond milk to reach your desired consistency.

3. Add the ice cubes and blend again until well combined and chilled.

4. Taste the shake and, if desired, add honey or maple syrup to sweeten it to your liking. Blend once more to mix in the sweetener.

5. Pour the peanut butter and jelly protein shake into a glass and enjoy your delicious, protein-packed breakfast!

Nutritional values: Calories: 360 kcal, Protein: 28 g, Carbohydrates: 35 g, Sugars: 18 g, Fiber: 6 g, Fat: 12 g, Saturated Fat: 2 g, Unsaturated Fat: 10 g, Cholesterol: 60 mg, Sodium: 250 mg

SMASHED AVOCADO TOAST WITH CHERRY TOMATOES

 PREP TIME: 10 MINUTES ✕ **SERVINGS: 1**

INGREDIENTS:

- 1 slice of whole-grain or whole-wheat bread
- 1/2 ripe avocado
- 1/4 cup cherry tomatoes, halved
- Salt and pepper, to taste
- Optional toppings: red pepper flakes, fresh basil, balsamic glaze, or crumbled feta cheese

DIRECTIONS:

1. Toast the whole-grain bread to your desired level of crispiness.
2. While the bread is toasting, cut the avocado in half, remove the pit, and scoop out the flesh into a small bowl. Using a fork, mash the avocado until it reaches your preferred consistency. Season with a pinch of salt and pepper to taste.
3. Spread the mashed avocado evenly on top of the toasted bread.
4. Arrange the halved cherry tomatoes on top of the avocado layer.
5. Add any optional toppings, such as a sprinkle of red pepper flakes for heat, a few fresh basil leaves for extra flavor, a drizzle of balsamic glaze for sweetness, or crumbled feta cheese for a salty touch.
6. Enjoy your delicious and nutritious smashed avocado toast with cherry tomatoes!

Nutritional values: Calories: 300 kcal, Protein: 9 g, Carbohydrates: 32 g, Sugars: 5 g, Fiber: 9 g, Fat: 17 g, Saturated Fat: 2.5 g, Unsaturated Fat: 14.5 g, Sodium: 250 mg

BLUEBERRY ALMOND OVERNIGHT OATS

 PREP TIME: 5 MINUTES (PLUS AT LEAST 4 HOURS OF CHILLING TIME) **SERVINGS: 1**

INGREDIENTS:

- 1/2 cup rolled oats
- 1/2 cup unsweetened almond milk (or milk of your choice)
- 1/2 cup fresh or frozen blueberries
- 1/4 cup Greek yogurt (plain or vanilla)
- 1 tbsp honey or maple syrup (optional)
- 1 tbsp chopped almonds
- 1/2 tsp vanilla extract
- Pinch of salt

DIRECTIONS:

1. In a mason jar or airtight container, combine the rolled oats, almond milk, blueberries, Greek yogurt, honey or maple syrup (if using), chopped almonds, vanilla extract, and a pinch of salt. Stir well to combine.
2. Seal the container with a lid or plastic wrap, and refrigerate for at least 4 hours or overnight for best results. The oats will absorb the liquid and soften, creating a creamy, pudding-like texture.
3. When ready to eat, stir the overnight oats well enough to mix in any settled ingredients.
4. Enjoy your delicious and nutritious overnight oats with blueberries and almonds straight from the jar, or transfer them to a bowl!

Nutritional values: Calories: 350 kcal, Protein: 13 g, Carbohydrates: 50 g, Sugars: 17 g, Fiber: 7 g, Fat: 11 g, Saturated Fat: 1.5 g, Unsaturated Fat: 9.5 g, Cholesterol: 5 mg, Sodium: 150 mg

BANANA AND NUT BUTTER RICE CAKE

 PREP TIME: 5 MINUTES **SERVINGS: 1**

INGREDIENTS:

- 2 brown rice cakes
- 2 tbsp natural nut butter (peanut, almond, or cashew)
- 1 medium banana, sliced
- Optional toppings: honey, cinnamon, or chia seeds

DIRECTIONS:

1. Lay the brown rice cakes on a plate or clean surface.
2. Spread 1 tbsp of your preferred nut butter evenly onto each rice cake.
3. Slice the banana into thin rounds and arrange them on top of the nut butter layer on each rice cake.
4. Add your favorite toppings, such as a drizzle of honey for extra sweetness, a sprinkle of cinnamon for a warm spice, or a few chia seeds for added texture and nutrition.
5. Enjoy your quick and delicious banana and nut butter rice cake breakfast!

Nutritional values: Calories: 360 kcal, Protein: 9 g, Carbohydrates: 48 g, Sugars: 17 g, Fiber: 6 g, Fat: 16 g, Saturated Fat: 2.5 g, Unsaturated Fat: 13.5 g, Sodium: 150 mg

VEGGIE SCRAMBLED EGG WRAP

 PREP TIME: 15 MINUTES   **SERVINGS: 1**

INGREDIENTS:

- 2 large eggs
- 1 tbsp olive oil or cooking spray
- 1/4 cup diced bell pepper (any color)
- 1/4 cup diced onion
- 1/4 cup chopped fresh spinach
- 1 whole-wheat tortilla (8-inch)
- Salt and pepper, to taste
- Optional toppings: hot sauce, salsa, shredded cheese, or avocado slices

DIRECTIONS:

1. In a small bowl, whisk the eggs and season with a pinch of salt and pepper. Set aside.

2. Heat the olive oil or cooking spray in a non-stick skillet over medium heat. Add the diced bell pepper and onion to the skillet and sauté for 3-4 minutes until the vegetables are softened and slightly golden.

3. Add the chopped spinach to the skillet and cook for 1-2 minutes until wilted.

4. Pour the whisked eggs into the skillet with the veggies and stir gently to combine. Cook for 2-3 minutes, occasionally stirring, until the eggs are fully cooked and scrambled.

5. Warm the whole-wheat tortilla in a separate skillet or microwave for 10-15 seconds to make it more pliable.

6. Transfer the scrambled egg and veggie mixture onto the center of the warmed tortilla. Add any optional toppings, such as hot sauce, salsa, shredded cheese, or avocado slices.

7. Fold the sides of the tortilla inward and roll it up tightly, enclosing the filling. Slice the wrap in half and enjoy your delicious, protein-packed, veggie scrambled egg wrap!

Nutritional values: Calories: 430 kcal, Protein: 20 g, Carbohydrates: 38 g, Sugars: 5 g, Fiber: 6 g, Fat: 22 g, Saturated Fat: 5 g, Unsaturated Fat: 17 g, Cholesterol: 370 mg, Sodium: 450 mg

PART II: WEEKEND BREAKFAST TREATS

CINNAMON ROLL PANCAKES WITH CREAM CHEESE GLAZE

 PREP TIME: 25 MINUTES   **SERVINGS: 4 (2 PANCAKES PER SERVING)**

INGREDIENTS:

For the pancakes:
- 2 cups all-purpose flour
- 2 tbsp granulated sugar
- 2 tsp baking powder
- 1/2 tsp salt
- 2 cups milk
- 2 large eggs
- 1 tsp vanilla extract
- Cooking spray or butter

For the cinnamon swirl:
- 1/4 cup unsalted butter, melted
- 1/2 cup packed light brown sugar
- 1 tbsp ground cinnamon

For the cream cheese glaze:
- 2 oz cream cheese, softened
- 1/4 cup powdered sugar
- 3 tbsp milk
- 1/2 tsp vanilla extract

DIRECTIONS:

1. Whisk the flour, sugar, baking powder, and salt in a large mixing bowl.

2. Mix the milk, eggs, and vanilla extract in a separate bowl. Gradually add the wet mixture to the dry ingredients, whisking until combined. Let the batter rest for 5 minutes.

3. Prepare the cinnamon swirl in a small bowl by combining the melted butter, brown sugar, and cinnamon. Transfer the mixture to a piping or zip-top plastic bag with a small corner cut off.

4. Preheat a non-stick skillet or griddle over medium heat and lightly coat with cooking spray or butter.

5. Pour about 1/4 cup of pancake batter onto the skillet. Pipe a spiral of the cinnamon swirl onto the pancake, starting from the center and working outwards. Cook the pancake for 2-3 minutes, until bubbles form on the surface, then flip and cook for another 2 minutes or until golden brown. Repeat with the remaining batter and cinnamon swirl.

6. To make the cream cheese glaze, beat the softened cream cheese, powdered sugar, milk, and vanilla extract together in a bowl until smooth and creamy.

7. Serve the pancakes warm, drizzled with the cream cheese glaze.

Nutritional values: Calories: 590 kcal, Protein: 13 g, Carbohydrates: 87 g, Sugars: 44 g, Fiber: 3 g, Fat: 22 g, Saturated Fat: 12 g, Unsaturated Fat: 10 g, Cholesterol: 135 mg, Sodium: 520 mg

VEGGIE AND CHEESE STUFFED OMELETTE

 PREP TIME: 20 MINUTES    **SERVINGS: 2**

INGREDIENTS:

- 4 large eggs
- 1/4 cup milk
- Salt and pepper, to taste
- 2 tbsp olive oil or cooking spray
- 1/4 cup diced bell pepper (any color)
- 1/4 cup diced onion
- 1/4 cup chopped fresh spinach
- 1/4 cup grated cheddar cheese (or cheese of your choice)
- Optional toppings: hot sauce, salsa, or avocado slices

DIRECTIONS:

1. Whisk together the eggs, milk, and a pinch of salt and pepper in a medium bowl. Set aside.

2. Heat 1 tbsp of olive oil or cooking spray in a non-stick skillet over medium heat. Add the diced bell pepper and onion to the skillet and sauté for 3-4 minutes until the vegetables are softened and slightly golden.

3. Add the chopped spinach to the skillet and cook for 1-2 minutes until wilted. Transfer the cooked veggies to a plate and set aside.

4. Wipe the skillet clean and heat the remaining 1 tbsp of olive oil or cooking spray over medium-low heat. Pour the egg mixture into the skillet and cook for 4-5 minutes until the edges are set and the center is slightly firm but moist.

5. Sprinkle half of the omelet with the cooked veggies and grated cheese. Carefully fold the other half of the omelet over the filling, pressing down gently with a spatula.

6. Cook for an additional 1-2 minutes to allow the cheese to melt. Slide the omelet onto a plate and cut it in half to serve.

7. Garnish the packed omelet with your preferred toppings, such as spicy sauce, salsa, or avocado slices.

Nutritional values: Calories: 360 kcal, Protein: 20 g, Carbohydrates: 8 g, Sugars: 4 g, Fiber: 1 g, Fat: 28 g, Saturated Fat: 9 g, Unsaturated Fat: 19 g, Cholesterol: 400 mg, Sodium: 350 mg

BANANA NUT FRENCH TOAST BAKE

 PREP TIME: 20 MINUTES (PLUS OVERNIGHT CHILLING)   **SERVINGS: 6**   **COOK TIME: 35 MINUTES**

INGREDIENTS:

- 1 loaf of day-old French bread (about 12 oz), cut into 1-inch cubes
- 4 large eggs
- 1 cup milk
- 1/2 cup heavy cream
- 1/2 cup granulated sugar
- 1/2 cup packed light brown sugar
- 2 tsp vanilla extract
- 1/2 tsp ground cinnamon
- 1/4 tsp ground nutmeg
- 2 ripe bananas, sliced
- 1/2 cup chopped walnuts

DIRECTIONS:

1. Grease a 9x13-inch baking dish and arrange the cubed French bread in the dish.
2. Whisk together the eggs, milk, heavy cream, granulated sugar, brown sugar, vanilla extract, cinnamon, and nutmeg in a large bowl. Pour the mixture evenly over the bread cubes, ensuring all pieces are soaked.
3. Arrange the banana slices on top of the bread, gently pressing them into the mixture. Sprinkle the chopped walnuts over the bananas.
4. Cover the baking dish with plastic wrap and refrigerate overnight, or for at least 4 hours, to allow the bread to fully absorb the liquid.
5. Preheat the oven to 350°F (180°C) when ready to bake.
6. Remove the plastic wrap and bake the French toast for 35-40 minutes until golden brown and set in the center. Cover the dish with aluminum foil if the top starts to brown too quickly.
7. Let the banana nut French toast bake cool for 5 minutes before serving. Enjoy with maple syrup, whipped cream, or fresh fruit.

Nutritional values: Calories: 540 kcal, Protein: 16 g, Carbohydrates: 74 g, Sugars: 38 g, Fiber: 4 g, Fat: 20 g, Saturated Fat: 7 g, Unsaturated Fat: 13 g, Cholesterol: 155 mg, Sodium: 470 mg

HUEVOS RANCHEROS WITH FRESH SALSA AND AVOCADO

 PREP TIME: 25 MINUTES    **SERVINGS: 4**    **COOK TIME: 15 MINUTES**

INGREDIENTS:

For the fresh salsa:
- 1 cup diced tomatoes
- 1/4 cup diced red onion
- 1/4 cup chopped fresh cilantro
- 1 jalapeño pepper, seeded and minced
- Juice of 1 lime
- Salt, to taste

For the huevos rancheros:
- 4 corn tortillas
- Cooking spray or olive oil
- 4 large eggs
- 1 cup canned black beans, rinsed and drained
- 1 avocado, pitted and sliced
- Salt and pepper, to taste
- Optional toppings: crumbled queso fresco, sour cream, or hot sauce

DIRECTIONS:

1. Prepare the fresh salsa by combining the diced tomatoes, red onion, cilantro, jalapeño pepper, and lime juice in a bowl. Season with salt to taste and set aside.

2. Preheat the oven to 350°F (180°C). Place the corn tortillas on a baking sheet and lightly spray or brush both sides with cooking spray or olive oil. Bake for 5-7 minutes until slightly crispy, turning once. Set aside.

3. In a large non-stick skillet over medium heat, cook the eggs to your desired level of doneness (e.g., sunny side up, over easy, or over hard). Season with salt and pepper.

4. To assemble the huevos rancheros, place one tortilla on each plate. Add avocado slices to the side and sprinkle with crumbled queso fresco. Layer with black beans, one cooked egg, and a generous spoonful of fresh salsa.

5. Serve immediately with optional toppings, such as sour cream or hot sauce, on the side.

Nutritional values: Calories: 370 kcal, Protein: 16 g, Carbohydrates: 40 g, Sugars: 4 g, Fiber: 11 g, Fat: 18 g, Saturated Fat: 3.5 g, Unsaturated Fat: 14.5 g, Cholesterol: 185 mg, Sodium: 320 mg

CHOCOLATE CHIP AND WALNUT BELGIAN WAFFLES

 PREP TIME: 15 MINUTES   SERVINGS: 4    COOK TIME: 20 MINUTES

INGREDIENTS:

- 2 cups all-purpose flour
- 2 tsp baking powder
- 1/2 tsp salt
- 2 cups milk
- 2 large eggs separated
- 1/2 cup unsalted butter, melted
- 1 tsp vanilla extract
- 3/4 cup chocolate chips
- 1/2 cup chopped walnuts
- Cooking spray or additional butter for the waffle iron
- Optional toppings: maple syrup, whipped cream, or fresh berries

DIRECTIONS:

1. Preheat your Belgian waffle iron according to the manufacturer's instructions.
2. Whisk together the flour, baking powder, and salt in a large bowl. Set aside.
3. In a separate bowl, mix the milk, egg yolks, melted butter, and vanilla extract. Gradually add the wet mixture to the dry ingredients, whisking until combined.
4. In another bowl, use an electric mixer to beat the egg whites until stiff peaks form. Gently fold the beaten egg whites into the batter, being careful not to overmix.
5. Fold the chocolate chips and chopped walnuts into the batter.
6. Lightly coat the waffle iron with cooking spray or butter. Pour the recommended amount of batter onto the hot waffle iron (usually about 1 cup) and close the lid. Cook the waffle until golden brown and crisp, following the manufacturer's instructions (usually 4-5 minutes).
7. Carefully remove the waffle from the iron and repeat with the remaining batter.
8. Serve the chocolate chip and walnut Belgian waffles warm, topped with your choice of maple syrup, whipped cream, or fresh berries.

Nutritional values: Calories: 780 kcal, Protein: 19 g, Carbohydrates: 87 g, Sugars: 32 g, Fiber: 4 g, Fat: 43 g, Saturated Fat: 20 g, Unsaturated Fat: 23 g, Cholesterol: 155 mg, Sodium: 680 mg

SPINACH, MUSHROOM, AND FETA QUICHE

 PREP TIME: 15 MINUTES   ✕ **SERVINGS: 6**   🕐 **COOK TIME: 45 MINUTES**

INGREDIENTS:

- 1 pre-made 9-inch pie crust (or homemade)
- 1 tbsp olive oil
- 1/2 cup diced onion
- 2 cups fresh spinach, chopped
- 1 cup sliced mushrooms
- 4 large eggs
- 1 cup milk
- 1/2 tsp salt
- 1/4 tsp black pepper
- 1/4 tsp ground nutmeg
- 1 cup crumbled feta cheese

DIRECTIONS:

1. Preheat the oven to 375°F (190°C). Press the pie crust into a 9-inch pie dish and set aside.
2. In a large skillet over medium heat, heat the olive oil. Add the diced onion and cook for 3-4 minutes until softened. Add the chopped spinach and cook until wilted about 2 minutes. Add the sliced mushrooms and cook for an additional 3-4 minutes until tender. Remove the skillet from the heat and let the vegetables cool slightly.
3. Whisk together the eggs, milk, salt, pepper, and nutmeg in a large bowl. Stir in the crumbled feta cheese.
4. Spread the cooked spinach and mushroom mixture evenly over the pie crust. Pour the egg mixture on top.
5. Bake the quiche for 40-45 minutes until the center is set and the crust is golden brown. If the edges of the crust begin to brown too quickly, cover them with aluminum foil.
6. Remove the quiche from the oven and let it cool for 5 minutes before slicing and serving.

Nutritional values: Calories: 330 kcal, Protein: 13 g, Carbohydrates: 21 g, Sugars: 3 g, Fiber: 1 g, Fat: 21 g, Saturated Fat: 9 g, Unsaturated Fat: 12 g, Cholesterol: 155 mg, Sodium: 620 mg

BLUEBERRY LEMON RICOTTA PANCAKES

 PREP TIME: 15 MINUTES

 COOK TIME: 20 MINUTES

 **SERVINGS: 4 (3 PANCAKES PER SERVING)**

INGREDIENTS:

- 1 1/2 cups all-purpose flour
- 1/4 cup granulated sugar
- 2 tsp baking powder
- 1/2 tsp salt
- 1 cup whole milk ricotta cheese
- 3/4 cup milk
- 3 large eggs separated
- Zest of 1 lemon
- 1 tsp vanilla extract
- 1 cup fresh blueberries
- Cooking spray or butter
- Optional toppings: powdered sugar, maple syrup, or lemon wedges

DIRECTIONS:

1. In a large bowl, whisk together the flour, sugar, baking powder, and salt. Set aside.

2. Mix the ricotta cheese, milk, egg yolks, lemon zest, and vanilla extract in a separate bowl. Gradually add the wet mixture to the dry ingredients, whisking until just combined.

3. In another bowl, beat the egg whites with an electric mixer until stiff peaks form. Gently fold the beaten egg whites into the pancake batter.

4. Preheat a non-stick skillet or griddle over medium heat and lightly coat with cooking spray or butter.

5. Pour about 1/4 cup of pancake batter onto the skillet for each pancake. Sprinkle a few blueberries onto each pancake. Cook for 2-3 minutes, or until bubbles form on the surface, then flip and cook for an additional 2 minutes, or until golden brown. Repeat with the remaining batter and blueberries.

6. Serve warm blueberry lemon ricotta pancakes, dusted with powdered sugar, drizzled with maple syrup, or with lemon wedges on the side.

Nutritional values: Calories: 460 kcal, Protein: 18 g, Carbohydrates: 58 g, Sugars: 20 g, Fiber: 2 g, Fat: 17 g, Saturated Fat: 9 g, Unsaturated Fat: 8 g, Cholesterol: 185 mg, Sodium: 590 mg

SMOKED SALMON AND CREAM CHEESE BAGELS

 PREP TIME: 10 MINUTES    **SERVINGS: 4**

INGREDIENTS:

- 4 plain or everything bagels, sliced in half
- 8 oz cream cheese, softened
- 8 oz smoked salmon
- 1/2 small red onion, thinly sliced
- 1 medium tomato, thinly sliced
- 1/2 English cucumber, thinly sliced
- 1/4 cup capers, drained
- Fresh dill sprigs for garnish
- Freshly ground black pepper, to taste

DIRECTIONS:

1. Toast the bagel halves to your desired level of crispiness.
2. Generously spread cream cheese on each toasted bagel half.
3. Arrange a layer of smoked salmon on top of the cream cheese.
4. Add a few slices of red onion, tomato, and cucumber to each bagel half.
5. Sprinkle capers over the assembled bagels and garnish with fresh dill sprigs.
6. Finish with a grind of freshly ground black pepper and serve immediately.

Nutritional values: Calories: 510 kcal, Protein: 26 g, Carbohydrates: 58 g, Sugars: 8 g, Fiber: 3 g, Fat: 20 g, Saturated Fat: 9 g, Unsaturated Fat: 11 g, Cholesterol: 60 mg, Sodium: 1450 mg

EGGS BENEDICT WITH HOMEMADE HOLLANDAISE SAUCE

 PREP TIME: 30 MINUTES   **SERVINGS: 4**   **COOK TIME: 10 MINUTES**

INGREDIENTS:

For the hollandaise sauce:
- 3 large egg yolks
- 1 tbsp water
- 1 tbsp lemon juice
- 1/2 cup unsalted butter, melted
- Salt and cayenne pepper, to taste

For the eggs benedict:
- 4 English muffins, split and toasted
- 8 slices Canadian bacon or ham
- 8 large eggs, poached
- Freshly chopped chives or parsley, for garnish

DIRECTIONS:

1. To make the hollandaise sauce, whisk together the egg yolks, water, and lemon juice in a heatproof bowl. Place the bowl over a pot of simmering water, making sure the bowl doesn't touch the water.

2. Continue whisking the egg yolk mixture until it starts to thicken, about 3-4 minutes. Gradually whisk in the melted butter in a slow, steady stream until fully incorporated and the sauce is thick and creamy. Remove the bowl from the heat and season with salt and cayenne pepper to taste. Keep the sauce warm by covering the bowl with a lid or aluminum foil.

3. Toast the English muffins and place two halves on each serving plate.

4. In a non-stick skillet over medium heat, cook the Canadian bacon or ham for 1-2 minutes per side until lightly browned and warmed through. Place one slice on top of each English muffin half.

5. To poach the eggs, fill a saucepan with water and bring it to a gentle simmer. Crack each egg into a small bowl and gently slide it into the simmering water. Cook the eggs for 3-4 minutes until the whites are set, and the yolks are still soft.

6. Use a slotted spoon to remove the poached eggs from the water and place one egg on top of each Canadian bacon slice.

7. Spoon a generous amount of hollandaise sauce over each egg and garnish with chopped chives or parsley. Serve the eggs benedict immediately.

Nutritional values: Calories: 660 kcal, Protein: 34 g, Carbohydrates: 38 g, Sugars: 3 g, Fiber: 2 g, Fat: 42 g, Saturated Fat: 20 g, Unsaturated Fat: 22 g, Cholesterol: 530 mg, Sodium: 1120 mg

SHAKSHUKA WITH FETA AND FRESH HERBS

 PREP TIME: 15 MINUTES　　 **SERVINGS: 4**　　 **COOK TIME: 25 MINUTES**

INGREDIENTS:

- 2 tbsp olive oil
- 1 medium onion, chopped
- 1 red bell pepper, chopped
- 3 garlic cloves, minced
- 1 tsp ground cumin
- 1 tsp paprika
- 1/4 tsp cayenne pepper (optional)
- 1 can (28 oz) crushed tomatoes
- Salt and pepper, to taste
- 4 large eggs
- 1/2 cup crumbled feta cheese
- 1/4 cup chopped fresh parsley
- 1/4 cup chopped fresh cilantro

DIRECTIONS:

1. Heat the olive oil in a large skillet over medium heat. Add the chopped onion and bell pepper, and cook for 5-7 minutes, occasionally stirring, until softened.

2. Add the minced garlic, cumin, paprika, and cayenne pepper (if using) to the skillet. Cook for 1-2 minutes until fragrant.

3. Stir in the crushed tomatoes and season with salt and pepper. Simmer the sauce for 10 minutes, occasionally stirring, until slightly thickened.

4. Use a spoon to make four small wells in the sauce. Crack an egg into each well, keeping the yolks intact. Season the eggs with salt and pepper.

5. Cover the skillet and cook for 5-8 minutes, or until the egg whites are set, and the yolks are still slightly runny (or cooked to your desired level of doneness).

6. Sprinkle the shakshuka with crumbled feta cheese, chopped parsley, and cilantro. Serve hot with crusty bread or pita for dipping.

Nutritional values: Calories: 290 kcal, Protein: 14 g, Carbohydrates: 20 g, Sugars: 11 g, Fiber: 5 g, Fat: 18 g, Saturated Fat: 6 g, Unsaturated Fat: 12 g, Cholesterol: 195 mg, Sodium: 530 mg

STRAWBERRY AND NUTELLA STUFFED CROISSANTS

 PREP TIME: 20 MINUTES   **SERVINGS: 4**   **COOK TIME: 15 MINUTES**

INGREDIENTS:

- 1 sheet puff pastry, thawed
- 4 tbsp Nutella (or other chocolate-hazelnut spread)
- 8 large strawberries, hulled and sliced
- 1 egg, lightly beaten
- 2 tbsp granulated sugar

DIRECTIONS:

1. Preheat the oven to 400°F (200°C) and line a baking sheet with parchment paper.

2. Roll out the puff pastry on a lightly floured surface into a 12x12-inch square. Cut the pastry into 4 equal squares.

3. Spoon 1 tbsp of Nutella into the center of each pastry square. Arrange 4-5 strawberry slices on top of the Nutella.

4. Fold the pastry squares diagonally to form a triangle, enclosing the Nutella and strawberries. Press the edges firmly with a fork to seal.

5. Transfer the stuffed croissants to the prepared baking sheet. Brush the tops with the beaten egg and sprinkle with granulated sugar.

6. Bake for 15-18 minutes or until the croissants are puffed and golden brown.

7. Allow the strawberry and Nutella stuffed croissants to cool for a few minutes before serving. Enjoy warm or at room temperature.

Nutritional values: Calories: 420 kcal, Protein: 6 g, Carbohydrates: 45 g, Sugars: 19 g, Fiber: 3 g, Fat: 24 g, Saturated Fat: 10 g, Unsaturated Fat: 14 g, Cholesterol: 55 mg, Sodium: 260 mg

BAKED APPLE CINNAMON OATMEAL

 PREP TIME: 15 MINUTES   **SERVINGS: 6**   **COOK TIME: 35 MINUTES**

INGREDIENTS:

- 2 cups rolled oats
- 1 tsp baking powder
- 1 1/2 tsp ground cinnamon
- 1/4 tsp ground nutmeg
- 1/4 tsp salt
- 1/4 cup packed light brown sugar
- 2 cups milk
- 1 large egg
- 2 tsp vanilla extract
- 2 tbsp unsalted butter, melted
- 1 1/2 cups diced apples (about 2 medium apples)
- Optional toppings: maple syrup, chopped nuts, or fresh berries

DIRECTIONS:

1. Preheat the oven to 375°F (190°C). Grease an 8x8-inch baking dish and set aside.
2. In a medium bowl, combine the rolled oats, baking powder, cinnamon, nutmeg, salt, and brown sugar. Stir until well mixed.
3. Whisk the milk, egg, and vanilla extract together in a separate bowl. Gradually add the wet mixture to the dry ingredients, stirring until well combined. Stir in the melted butter.
4. Fold in the diced apples and pour the oatmeal mixture into the prepared baking dish, spreading it evenly.
5. Bake for 35-40 minutes, or until the top is golden brown and the oatmeal is set.
6. Remove from the oven and let the baked apple cinnamon oatmeal cool for 5 minutes before serving. Serve warm with optional toppings like maple syrup, chopped nuts, or fresh berries.

Nutritional values: Calories: 280 kcal, Protein: 8 g, Carbohydrates: 42 g, Sugars: 17 g, Fiber: 4 g, Fat: 9 g, Saturated Fat: 4.5 g, Unsaturated Fat: 4.5 g, Cholesterol: 50 mg, Sodium: 210 mg

LUNCH – ENERGIZING YOUR COLLEGE ADVENTURE

Now that we've tackled the day's most important meal let's move on to lunch. I know that college life is full of surprises, and you never know when you might have to pull an all-nighter or sprint between classes. That's where a good lunch comes in. Fueling your body and brain with the appropriate nutrients is critical to keep your energy levels high and your mind sharp. In this chapter of the College Students' Cookbook, we'll explore two different types of lunch ideas to keep you going, whether you're on the go or looking for something more substantial.

I. On-the-go lunches

These quick and portable lunch options are perfect when you're rushing from one class to another or want to grab something to eat before heading to the library. We've got you covered with three types of on-the-go lunches:

- Wraps and sandwiches: Quick to prepare, simple to eat, and adaptable to whatever combination of ingredients you choose.

- Salads in a jar: Layered salads that you can make beforehand and take in a mason jar. Simply shake it up and enjoy a fresh, invigorating lunch.

- Bento boxes: These portable meals in a box are not only convenient, but they're also a terrific method to keep your lunch balanced and portioned.

II. Hearty lunch bowls

Hearty lunch bowls are your solution when you need something more significant to get you through the day. These rich dishes can be prepared ahead of time and assembled quickly for a simple but filling lunch:

- Rice bowls: Begin with a rice base and then add your favorite protein, vegetables, and sauce for a wonderful and full meal.

- Grain bowls: Substitute quinoa, barley, or farro for the rice, then top with your favorite toppings for a nutrient-dense lunch.

- Noodle bowls: Warm up with a bowl of noodles, broth, and your preferred protein and vegetables. This one is great for those chilly campus days.

Funny story: while I was in college, I had this "lucky meal" that I always had before important exams. It was a basic chicken and avocado sandwich on whole-grain bread with baby carrots on the side. This lunch, I believe, strengthened my brain and kept me focused during my exams. Having a go-to lunch choice made me feel more prepared and confident, whether it was a superstition or not. So, you choose your own "lucky meal," as well, whether it's a wrap, a salad, or a big bowl, to keep you fuelled and ready to face whatever challenge college life throws your way!

WRAPS AND SANDWICHES

TURKEY, AVOCADO, AND HUMMUS WRAP

 PREP TIME: 10 MINUTES   **SERVINGS: 2**

INGREDIENTS:

- 2 large whole wheat tortillas
- 4 tbsp hummus
- 6 slices deli turkey breast
- 1 ripe avocado, pitted and sliced
- 1 cup baby spinach leaves
- 1/2 cup shredded carrots
- Salt and pepper, to taste

DIRECTIONS:

1. Lay out the whole wheat tortillas on a clean surface. Spread 2 tablespoons of hummus onto each tortilla, leaving a 1-inch border around the edges.
2. Arrange three slices of turkey breast on each tortilla, overlapping them slightly.
3. Layer the avocado slices on top of the turkey, followed by the baby spinach leaves and shredded carrots.
4. Season with salt and pepper to taste.
5. Roll up the wraps tightly, tucking in the sides as you go. Cut each wrap in half diagonally, and wrap in foil or plastic wrap if taken on the go.

Nutritional values: Calories: 460 kcal, Protein: 24 g, Carbohydrates: 42 g, Sugars: 4 g, Fiber: 9 g, Fat: 23 g, Saturated Fat: 4 g, Unsaturated Fat: 19 g, Cholesterol: 40 mg, Sodium: 940 mg

CAPRESE SANDWICH

 PREP TIME: 10 MINUTES   **SERVINGS: 2**

INGREDIENTS:

- 4 slices of whole-grain bread
- 4 oz fresh mozzarella cheese, sliced
- 1 large ripe tomato, sliced
- 1/4 cup fresh basil leaves
- 2 tbsp balsamic glaze
- 1 tbsp olive oil
- Salt and freshly ground black pepper to taste

Nutritional values: Calories: 450 kcal, Protein: 18 g, Carbohydrates: 49 g, Sugars: 12 g, Fiber: 6 g, Fat: 20 g, Saturated Fat: 8 g, Unsaturated Fat: 12 g, Cholesterol: 40 mg, Sodium: 600 mg

DIRECTIONS:

1. Lay out the slices of bread on a cutting board or clean surface.
2. Arrange the sliced mozzarella cheese on two of the bread slices.
3. Top the cheese with sliced tomatoes, followed by a sprinkling of salt and freshly ground black pepper to taste.
4. Add a layer of fresh basil leaves over the tomatoes.
5. Drizzle the balsamic glaze and olive oil over the basil leaves.
6. Top each sandwich with the remaining slices of bread.
7. Cut the sandwiches in half, if desired, and serve immediately.

BBQ CHICKEN AND COLESLAW WRAP

 PREP TIME: 20 MINUTES   **SERVINGS: 4**   **COOK TIME: 10 MINUTES**

INGREDIENTS:

- 2 cups shredded cooked chicken (rotisserie chicken works great)
- 1/2 cup BBQ sauce, plus more for drizzling (store-bought or homemade)
- 2 cups coleslaw mix (prepackaged or shredded cabbage and carrots)
- 1/4 cup mayonnaise
- 2 tbsp apple cider vinegar
- 1 tbsp sugar
- Salt and pepper, to taste
- 4 large whole wheat tortillas
- 1/2 cup shredded cheddar cheese (optional)

DIRECTIONS:

1. Mix the shredded cooked chicken in a medium-sized bowl with 1/2 cup of BBQ sauce until well-coated. Set aside.

2. In another medium-sized bowl, combine the coleslaw mix, mayonnaise, apple cider vinegar, sugar, salt, and pepper. Stir well to combine, and let the mixture sit for 5 minutes to allow the flavors to meld.

3. Warm the tortillas in the microwave for 15-20 seconds or on a hot pan for 30 seconds per side to make them more pliable.

4. To assemble the wraps, lay out the tortillas on a flat surface. Divide the BBQ chicken mixture evenly among the tortillas, placing it in the center. Top with the coleslaw and shredded cheddar cheese, if using.

5. Fold the sides of the tortilla inward, then roll the tortilla up tightly, starting from the bottom to create a wrap. If desired, drizzle additional BBQ sauce on top before closing the wrap.

6. Cut the wraps in half diagonally and serve immediately.

Nutritional values: Calories: 450 kcal, Protein: 28 g, Carbohydrates: 44 g, Sugars: 12 g, Fiber: 5 g, Fat: 18 g, Saturated Fat: 5 g, Unsaturated Fat: 13 g, Cholesterol: 65 mg, Sodium: 1200 mg

VEGGIE PESTO PANINI

 PREP TIME: 10 MINUTES  **SERVINGS: 2**  **COOK TIME: 5 MINUTES**

INGREDIENTS:

- 4 slices of whole-grain bread
- 1/4 cup basil pesto
- 1 small zucchini, sliced into thin rounds
- 1 small red bell pepper, sliced into thin strips
- 1/4 red onion, thinly sliced
- 1/2 cup fresh spinach leaves
- 4 slices provolone or mozzarella cheese
- Olive oil for the panini press

Nutritional values: Calories: 480 kcal, Protein: 22 g, Carbohydrates: 45 g, Sugars: 6 g, Fiber: 6 g, Fat: 24 g, Saturated Fat: 9 g, Unsaturated Fat: 15 g, Cholesterol: 35 mg, Sodium: 720 mg

DIRECTIONS:

1. Preheat your panini press on medium heat.
2. Spread a thin layer of basil pesto on one side of each slice of bread.
3. Layer zucchini, red bell pepper, red onion, spinach, and cheese slices on top of the pesto on two bread slices.
4. Top with the remaining two bread slices, pesto side down, to create two sandwiches.
5. Lightly brush the panini press with olive oil.
6. Place the sandwiches on the panini press or grill pan and close the press. Cook for about 5 minutes until the bread is golden and crispy and the cheese is melted.
7. Remove the paninis from the press, and let them rest for a minute before slicing them in half. Serve immediately.

CHIPOTLE CHICKEN AND CHEESE SANDWICH

 PREP TIME: 10 MINUTES **SERVINGS: 2** **COOK TIME: 5 MINUTES**

INGREDIENTS:

- 4 slices whole-grain bread
- 1 cup cooked and shredded chicken breast
- 1/4 cup canned chipotle peppers in adobo sauce, chopped
- 1/4 cup light mayonnaise
- 1/2 cup shredded cheddar cheese
- 1 small tomato, sliced
- 1 cup fresh baby spinach leaves
- Butter or cooking spray for grilling

Nutritional values: Calories: 540 kcal, Protein: 35 g, Carbohydrates: 45 g, Sugars: 6 g, Fiber: 6 g, Fat: 24 g, Saturated Fat: 9 g, Unsaturated Fat: 15 g, Cholesterol: 90 mg, Sodium: 930 mg

DIRECTIONS:

1. Combine the shredded chicken, chopped chipotle peppers, and light mayonnaise in a small bowl. Mix well until the chicken is evenly coated.
2. Lay out the slices of whole-grain bread. On two of the slices, evenly distribute the chipotle chicken mixture. Top with shredded cheddar cheese, tomato slices, and baby spinach leaves. Place the remaining bread slices on top to form the sandwiches.
3. Heat a pan or griddle over medium heat. Lightly butter or spray the cooking surface with cooking spray. Place the sandwiches on the pan and cook for 2-3 minutes per side until the cheese is melted. Press gently with a spatula to help the cheese melt evenly.
4. Remove the sandwiches from the pan, let them cool for a minute, then slice them in half and serve immediately.

MEDITERRANEAN FALAFEL WRAP

 PREP TIME: 15 MINUTES   **SERVINGS: 4**   **COOK TIME: 5 MINUTES (IF USING PRE-MADE FALAFEL)**

INGREDIENTS:

- 4 large whole wheat wraps
- 1 cup hummus
- 12 pre-made falafel balls, warmed according to package instructions (or homemade, if preferred)
- 1 cup chopped cucumber
- 1 cup chopped tomatoes
- 1/2 cup sliced red onion
- 1/2 cup pitted and chopped Kalamata olives
- 1/2 cup crumbled feta cheese
- 1/4 cup chopped fresh parsley
- Salt and pepper, to taste

DIRECTIONS:

1. Lay out the whole wheat wraps on a clean work surface. Spread about 1/4 cup of hummus on each wrap, leaving a border around the edges.
2. Divide the warmed falafel balls evenly among the wraps, placing them in the center of the hummus layer.
3. Top each wrap with an equal amount of cucumber, tomatoes, red onion, olives, feta cheese, and parsley—season with salt and pepper to taste.
4. Fold in the sides of each wrap and then roll them up tightly, enclosing the filling. Cut each wrap in half on a diagonal and serve immediately.

Nutritional values: Calories: 590 kcal, Protein: 22 g, Carbohydrates: 70 g, Sugars: 7 g, Fiber: 13 g, Fat: 27 g, Saturated Fat: 7 g, Unsaturated Fat: 20 g, Cholesterol: 25 mg, Sodium: 950 mg

SALADS IN A JAR

GREEK SALAD WITH LEMON VINAIGRETTE IN A JAR

 PREP TIME: 15 MINUTES    **SERVINGS: 2**

INGREDIENTS:

For the lemon vinaigrette:
- 3 tbsp olive oil
- 2 tbsp freshly squeezed lemon juice
- 1 tsp honey
- 1 small garlic clove, minced
- Salt and pepper, to taste

For the salad:
- 1 cup cherry tomatoes, halved
- 1 cup chopped cucumber
- 1/2 cup sliced red onion
- 1/2 cup pitted Kalamata olives
- 1/2 cup crumbled feta cheese
- 2 cups chopped Romaine lettuce
- 2 tbsp chopped fresh parsley

DIRECTIONS:

1. Prepare the lemon vinaigrette by whisking together the olive oil, lemon juice, honey, and minced garlic in a small bowl. Season with salt and pepper to taste. Set aside.

2. Divide the cherry tomatoes between two 1-liter mason jars, creating the first layer at the bottom of the jars.

3. Add a layer of chopped cucumber on top of the tomatoes, followed by layers of sliced red onion, Kalamata olives, and crumbled feta cheese.

4. Stuff the chopped Romaine lettuce into the jars on top of the feta cheese layer. Top each jar with a tablespoon of chopped fresh parsley.

5. Divide the lemon vinaigrette into two small, separate airtight containers. Seal the mason jars and the vinaigrette containers.

6. When ready to eat, pour the lemon vinaigrette over the salad in the jar, seal the jar, and shake well to mix. Pour the salad onto a plate or eat directly from the jar.

Nutritional values: Calories: 420 kcal, Protein: 10 g, Carbohydrates: 22 g, Sugars: 10 g, Fiber: 5 g, Fat: 33 g, Saturated Fat: 9 g, Unsaturated Fat: 24 g, Cholesterol: 35 mg, Sodium: 970 mg

COBB SALAD IN A JAR

 PREP TIME: 20 MINUTES  **SERVINGS: 2**

INGREDIENTS:

For the dressing:
- 1/4 cup plain Greek yogurt
- 2 tbsp olive oil
- 1 tbsp red wine vinegar
- 1 small garlic clove, minced
- Salt and pepper, to taste

For the salad:
- 1/2 cup cherry tomatoes, halved
- 1/2 cup cooked and chopped bacon
- 1/2 cup crumbled blue cheese
- 1/2 cup chopped avocado (about 1 small avocado)
- 1/2 cup cooked and chopped chicken breast
- 1/4 cup sliced green onions
- 4 hard-boiled eggs, peeled and quartered
- 4 cups chopped Romaine lettuce

DIRECTIONS:

1. Prepare the dressing in a small bowl by whisking together the Greek yogurt, olive oil, red wine vinegar, and minced garlic. Season with salt and pepper to taste. Set aside.

2. Divide the cherry tomatoes between two 1-liter mason jars, creating the first layer at the bottom of the jars.

3. Add a layer of chopped bacon on top of the tomatoes, followed by layers of crumbled blue cheese, chopped avocado, and cooked chicken breast.

4. Place a layer of sliced green onions and quartered hard-boiled eggs over the chicken.

5. Stuff the chopped Romaine lettuce into the jars on top of the egg layer.

6. Divide the dressing into two small, separate airtight containers. Seal the mason jars and the dressing containers.

7. When ready to eat, pour the dressing over the salad in the jar, seal the jar, and shake well to mix. Pour the salad onto a plate or eat directly from the jar.

Nutritional values: Calories: 650 kcal, Protein: 43 g, Carbohydrates: 15 g, Sugars: 6 g, Fiber: 6 g, Fat: 47 g, Saturated Fat: 14 g, Unsaturated Fat: 33 g, Cholesterol: 420 mg, Sodium: 1030 mg

QUINOA AND BLACK BEAN SALAD IN A JAR

 PREP TIME:20 MINUTES   **SERVINGS: 2**    **COOK TIME: 15 MINUTES (FOR QUINOA)**

INGREDIENTS:

For the lime vinaigrette:
- 3 tbsp olive oil
- 2 tbsp freshly squeezed lime juice
- 1 tsp honey
- 1 small garlic clove, minced
- Salt and pepper, to taste

For the salad:
- 1 cup cooked quinoa, cooled
- 1 cup canned black beans, rinsed and drained
- 1 cup corn kernels (fresh, frozen, or canned)
- 1 cup cherry tomatoes, halved
- 1 avocado, diced
- 1/4 cup chopped fresh cilantro
- 2 cups baby spinach

DIRECTIONS:

1. Prepare the lime vinaigrette by whisking together the olive oil, lime juice, honey, and minced garlic in a small bowl. Season with salt and pepper to taste. Set aside.

2. Divide the cooked and cooled quinoa between two 1-liter mason jars, creating the first layer at the bottom of the jars.

3. Add a layer of black beans to the quinoa, followed by layers of corn kernels, cherry tomatoes, diced avocado, and chopped cilantro.

4. Stuff the baby spinach into the jars on top of the cilantro layer.

5. Divide the lime vinaigrette into two small, separate airtight containers. Seal the mason jars and the vinaigrette containers.

6. When ready to eat, pour the lime vinaigrette over the salad in the jar, seal the jar, and shake well to mix. Pour the salad onto a plate or eat directly from the jar.

Nutritional values: Calories: 580 kcal, Protein: 18 g, Carbohydrates: 66 g, Sugars: 9 g, Fiber: 17 g, Fat: 30 g, Saturated Fat: 4.5 g, Unsaturated Fat: 25.5 g, Sodium: 280 mg

ASIAN CHICKEN NOODLE SALAD IN A JAR

 PREP TIME: 20 MINUTES

 **SERVINGS: 2**

 **COOK TIME: 10 MINUTES (FOR COOKING NOODLES AND CHICKEN)**

INGREDIENTS:

For the dressing:
- 3 tbsp rice vinegar
- 2 tbsp soy sauce
- 1 tbsp honey
- 1 tsp grated fresh ginger
- 1 small garlic clove, minced
- 1 tbsp sesame oil

For the salad:
- 4 oz cooked and cooled soba noodles (or other noodles of your choice)
- 1 cup cooked and shredded chicken breast
- 1 cup shredded red cabbage
- 1 cup julienned carrots
- 1/2 cup shelled edamame
- 1/4 cup thinly sliced green onions
- 1/4 cup chopped fresh cilantro
- 2 tbsp toasted sesame seeds

DIRECTIONS:

1. Prepare the dressing in a small bowl by whisking together the rice vinegar, soy sauce, honey, grated ginger, minced garlic, and sesame oil. Set aside.

2. Divide the dressing between two 1-liter mason jars, creating the first layer at the bottom of the jars.

3. Add a layer of cooked soba noodles on top of the dressing, followed by layers of shredded chicken, red cabbage, julienned carrots, edamame, green onions, and cilantro.

4. Seal the mason jars and store them in the refrigerator until ready to eat.

5. When ready to enjoy, shake the jar well to mix the dressing with the salad ingredients. Pour the salad onto a plate or eat directly from the jar, and sprinkle with toasted sesame seeds.

Nutritional values: Calories: 480 kcal, Protein: 32 g, Carbohydrates: 60 g, Sugars: 12 g, Fiber: 7 g, Fat: 15 g, Saturated Fat: 2.5 g, Unsaturated Fat: 12.5 g, Cholesterol: 65 mg, Sodium: 1010 mg

BENTO BOXES

SUSHI ROLL BENTO

 PREP TIME: 25 MINUTES    **SERVINGS: 2**    **COOK TIME: 20 MINUTES (FOR SUSHI RICE)**

INGREDIENTS:

For the sushi rice:
- 1 cup sushi rice
- 1 1/4 cups water
- 2 tbsp rice vinegar
- 1 tbsp sugar
- 1/2 tsp salt

For the sushi rolls:
- 2 sheets nori (seaweed)
- 1 small cucumber, julienned
- 1 small avocado, thinly sliced
- 1/2 cup cooked and shredded crab or imitation crab

For the bento box:
- 1 cup cherry tomatoes
- 1 cup edamame (in pods, cooked and cooled)
- 2 tbsp soy sauce for dipping (in small containers)
- 1 tbsp pickled ginger
- 1 tsp wasabi paste (optional)

DIRECTIONS:

1. Cook sushi rice according to the package instructions. Meanwhile, in a small saucepan, combine rice vinegar, sugar, and salt. Heat over low heat until the sugar dissolves. Set aside to cool.

2. When the rice is cooked, transfer it to a large bowl and let it cool slightly. Add the vinegar mixture to the rice and gently fold to combine. Let the rice cool completely.

3. Lay a sheet of nori on a bamboo sushi mat or plastic wrap. Spread half of the sushi rice evenly on the nori, leaving a 1/2-inch border at the top.

4. Place half of the cucumber, avocado, and crab in a line along the bottom edge of the rice layer. Using the sushi mat or plastic wrap, roll the sushi tightly, sealing the top edge with a little bit of water. Repeat with the remaining nori, rice, and fillings.

5. Cut each sushi roll into 6-8 pieces using a sharp knife. Arrange the sushi rolls in two bento boxes.

6. Add cherry tomatoes, edamame, pickled ginger, and wasabi (if using) to the bento boxes. Pack the soy sauce in small containers for dipping.

7. Keep the bento boxes refrigerated until ready to eat.

Nutritional values: Calories: 650 kcal, Protein: 25 g, Carbohydrates: 97 g, Sugars: 10 g, Fiber: 11 g, Fat: 20 g, Saturated Fat: 3 g, Unsaturated Fat: 17 g, Cholesterol: 30 mg, Sodium: 1290 mg

CHICKEN TERIYAKI BENTO BOX

 PREP TIME: 15 MINUTES   **SERVINGS: 4**   **COOK TIME: 15 MINUTES**

INGREDIENTS:

For the chicken teriyaki:
- 1 lb boneless, skinless chicken thighs cut into bite-sized pieces
- 1/4 cup low-sodium soy sauce
- 1/4 cup mirin (sweet rice wine)
- 1/4 cup sugar
- 1 tbsp cornstarch mixed with 2 tbsp water
- 1 tbsp vegetable oil

For the bento box:
- 2 cups cooked short-grain white rice divided
- 1 cup steamed broccoli florets, divided
- 1 cup julienned carrots divided
- 1/2 cup edamame, divided
- Optional: black sesame seeds for garnish

DIRECTIONS:

1. Combine the soy sauce, mirin, and sugar in a small saucepan. Bring to a simmer over medium heat, stirring until the sugar dissolves. Stir in the cornstarch mixture and cook, constantly stirring, until the sauce thickens. Remove from heat and set aside.

2. Heat the vegetable oil in a large skillet over medium-high heat. Add the chicken pieces and cook, occasionally stirring, until browned and cooked through, about 6-8 minutes.

3. Pour the teriyaki sauce over the chicken, stirring to coat the chicken evenly. Cook for 1-2 minutes until the chicken is glazed and heated.

4. To assemble the bento boxes, divide the cooked rice, steamed broccoli, julienned carrots, and edamame evenly among four bento box compartments or containers.

5. Top the rice with the chicken teriyaki, dividing it equally among the four bento boxes. Optionally, garnish the chicken with black sesame seeds.

6. Store the bento boxes in the refrigerator until ready to eat. Reheat the chicken and rice compartments in the microwave, if desired.

Nutritional values: Calories: 550 kcal, Protein: 35 g, Carbohydrates: 71 g, Sugars: 15 g, Fiber: 5 g, Fat: 15 g, Saturated Fat: 3 g, Unsaturated Fat: 12 g, Cholesterol: 105 mg, Sodium: 710 mg

VEGETARIAN QUINOA AND ROASTED VEGGIE BENTO

 PREP TIME: 20 MINUTES    **SERVINGS: 4**    **COOK TIME: 20 MINUTES**

INGREDIENTS:

- 2 cups cooked quinoa, cooled
- 2 cups broccoli florets
- 2 cups halved Brussels sprouts
- 2 cups chopped bell pepper (any color)
- 2 tbsp olive oil
- 1 cup cherry tomatoes, halved
- 1 cup edamame, shelled and cooked
- 1/4 cup chopped fresh parsley
- 1/4 cup sunflower seeds
- Salt and pepper

For the lemon-tahini dressing:

- 1/4 cup tahini
- 2 tbsp freshly squeezed lemon juice
- 2 tbsp water
- 1 tbsp olive oil
- 1 small garlic clove, minced
- Salt and pepper, to taste

DIRECTIONS:

1. Preheat the oven to 400°F (200°C). Line a baking sheet with parchment paper.

2. Place the broccoli florets, Brussels sprouts, and bell pepper on the prepared baking sheet. Drizzle with olive oil and season with salt and pepper. Toss to coat and spread the vegetables out in a single layer.

3. Roast the vegetables in the oven for 20-25 minutes or until tender and slightly browned. Remove from the oven and let them cool.

4. In a small bowl, prepare the lemon-tahini dressing by whisking the tahini, lemon juice, water, olive oil, and minced garlic. Season with salt and pepper to taste.

5. Assemble the bento boxes by dividing the cooked quinoa evenly among four bento box compartments or containers. Add equal portions of the roasted vegetables, cherry tomatoes, and edamame to each bento box.

6. Sprinkle each bento box with chopped parsley and sunflower seeds. Divide the lemon-tahini dressing into four small airtight containers, including one with each bento box.

7. When ready to eat, drizzle the lemon-tahini dressing over the quinoa and vegetables, and enjoy!

Nutritional values: Calories: 520 kcal, Protein: 20 g, Carbohydrates: 55 g, Sugars: 8 g, Fiber: 12 g, Fat: 28 g, Saturated Fat: 4 g, Unsaturated Fat: 24 g, Cholesterol: 0 mg, Sodium: 120 mg

SPICY TOFU POKE BOWL BENTO

 PREP TIME: 20 MINUTES   **SERVINGS: 2**    **COOK TIME: 25 MINUTES (FOR RICE)**

INGREDIENTS:

For the spicy tofu poke:
- 14 oz extra-firm tofu, pressed and cubed
- 3 tbsp soy sauce
- 2 tbsp rice vinegar
- 1 tbsp sesame oil
- 1 tbsp honey
- 1 tsp sriracha (or more, to taste)
- 1 green onion, finely chopped
- 1 tsp toasted sesame seeds

For the bento box:
- 1 cup uncooked sushi rice
- 2 cups water
- 1 tbsp rice vinegar
- 1 tsp sugar
- 1/2 tsp salt
- 1 cup steamed edamame
- 1 cup shredded purple cabbage
- 1 avocado, sliced
- Optional: pickled ginger and wasabi for serving

DIRECTIONS:

1. Prepare the sushi rice by rinsing it in cold water until it runs clear. Combine the rice and 2 cups of water in a medium saucepan. Bring to a boil, then reduce heat to low and cover. Cook for 20 minutes or until the rice has absorbed all the water. Remove from heat and let it stand for 10 minutes, covered.

2. Mix 1 tbsp rice vinegar, 1 tsp sugar, and 1/2 tsp salt in a small bowl. Gently fold the vinegar mixture into the cooked sushi rice, being careful not to mash the rice. Set aside to cool.

3. In a medium bowl, whisk together the soy sauce, rice vinegar, sesame oil, honey, and sriracha. Add the cubed tofu, green onion, and sesame seeds. Toss to coat the tofu in the sauce. Set aside to marinate for 10 minutes.

4. Assemble the bento boxes by dividing the cooled sushi rice between two bento box compartments. Add half of the spicy tofu poke to each bento box and equal portions of steamed edamame, shredded purple cabbage, and avocado slices.

5. If desired, include pickled ginger and wasabi in separate bento box compartments. Seal the bento boxes and refrigerate until ready to eat.

Nutritional values: Calories: 760 kcal, Protein: 34 g, Carbohydrates: 106 g, Sugars: 13 g, Fiber: 12 g, Fat: 24 g, Saturated Fat: 3.5 g, Unsaturated Fat: 20.5 g, Cholesterol: 0 mg, Sodium: 1280 mg

RICE BOWLS

VEGETARIAN MEXICAN RICE BOWL

 PREP TIME: 20 MINUTES   **SERVINGS: 4**   **COOK TIME: 20 MINUTES**

INGREDIENTS:

- 1 cup uncooked brown rice
- 2 cups vegetable broth or water
- 1 tbsp olive oil
- 1 small onion, diced
- 1 red bell pepper, diced
- 1 can (15 oz) black beans, rinsed and drained
- 1 cup frozen corn, thawed
- 1 can (14.5 oz) diced tomatoes, drained
- 1/2 tsp ground cumin
- 1/2 tsp chili powder
- Salt and pepper, to taste
- 1/4 cup chopped fresh cilantro
- 1 avocado, sliced
- Optional toppings: shredded cheese, sour cream, salsa, or hot sauce

DIRECTIONS:

1. In a medium saucepan, combine the brown rice and vegetable broth (or water). Bring to a boil, then reduce heat to low and cover. Cook for 20-25 minutes or until rice is tender and liquid is absorbed. Fluff with a fork and set aside.

2. In a large skillet, heat the olive oil over medium heat. Add the diced onion and bell pepper, and cook until softened about 5 minutes.

3. Stir in the black beans, corn, diced tomatoes, cumin, chili powder, salt, and pepper. Cook for another 5-7 minutes until heated through.

4. To assemble the rice bowls, divide the cooked rice among four bowls. Top with the vegetable and bean mixture, then sprinkle with chopped cilantro. Add avocado slices and any desired toppings, such as shredded cheese, sour cream, salsa, or hot sauce.

5. Serve immediately and enjoy!

Nutritional values: Calories: 430 kcal, Protein: 14 g, Carbohydrates: 71 g, Sugars: 6 g, Fiber: 14 g, Fat: 11 g, Saturated Fat: 1.5 g, Unsaturated Fat: 9.5 g, Sodium: 600 mg

TERIYAKI CHICKEN RICE BOWL

 PREP TIME: 20 MINUTES    **SERVINGS: 4**    **COOK TIME: 20 MINUTES**

INGREDIENTS:

- 1 lb boneless, skinless chicken breasts cut into bite-sized pieces
- 1/4 cup low-sodium soy sauce
- 1/4 cup honey
- 1/4 cup rice vinegar
- 1 tbsp minced garlic
- 1 tbsp minced ginger
- 1 tbsp cornstarch
- 2 cups cooked white or brown rice
- 2 cups steamed mixed vegetables (broccoli, bell peppers, carrots, etc.)
- 2 tbsp chopped green onions
- 1 tbsp sesame seeds

DIRECTIONS:

1. Whisk together the soy sauce, honey, rice vinegar, garlic, and ginger in a small bowl. Set aside.

2. In a large non-stick skillet over medium heat, cook the chicken pieces until they are browned and cooked through, about 6-8 minutes per side. Remove the chicken from the skillet and set aside.

3. Pour the teriyaki sauce mixture into the skillet and cook over medium heat until it starts to thicken, about 3-4 minutes. Mix the cornstarch with one tablespoon of water in a small bowl to create a slurry, then whisk it into the sauce. Continue to cook the sauce for another 2-3 minutes until it reaches your desired consistency.

4. Return the cooked chicken to the skillet and toss to coat it in the teriyaki sauce.

5. To assemble the rice bowls, divide the cooked rice among four bowls. Top each bowl with equal portions of teriyaki chicken and steamed vegetables. Sprinkle with chopped green onions and sesame seeds before serving.

Nutritional values: Calories: 460 kcal, Protein: 33 g, Carbohydrates: 60 g, Sugars: 19 g, Fiber: 3 g, Fat: 8 g, Saturated Fat: 1.5 g, Unsaturated Fat: 6.5 g, Cholesterol: 75 mg, Sodium: 600 mg

SPICY SHRIMP AND VEGGIE RICE BOWL

 PREP TIME: 15 MINUTES    **SERVINGS: 4**    **COOK TIME: 20 MINUTES**

INGREDIENTS:

- 1 cup uncooked jasmine or basmati rice
- 2 cups water
- 1 lb large shrimp, peeled and deveined
- 1 tbsp olive oil
- Salt and pepper, to taste
- 1 red bell pepper, sliced
- 1 yellow bell pepper, sliced
- 1 small red onion, sliced
- 2 cups broccoli florets
- 1/4 cup low-sodium soy sauce
- 2 tbsp sriracha sauce (adjust to taste)
- 1 tbsp honey
- 2 cloves garlic, minced
- 1 tsp grated fresh ginger
- Optional toppings: chopped green onions, sesame seeds, or lime wedges

DIRECTIONS:

1. In a medium saucepan, combine the rice and water. Bring to a boil, then reduce the heat to low and cover. Cook for 15-20 minutes until the rice is tender and the water is absorbed. Remove from heat and let stand, covered, for 5 minutes. Fluff with a fork.

2. Meanwhile, heat the olive oil in a large skillet over medium heat. Season the shrimp with salt and pepper and cook for 2-3 minutes per side or until pink and cooked through. Transfer to a plate and set aside.

3. Add bell peppers, red onion, and broccoli in the same skillet. Cook for 5-7 minutes or until the vegetables are tender-crisp. Remove from heat.

4. Whisk together the soy sauce, sriracha, honey, garlic, and ginger in a small bowl. Pour the sauce over the cooked vegetables and stir to coat.

5. To assemble the rice bowls, divide the cooked rice among four bowls. Top each bowl with an equal portion of the cooked vegetables and shrimp. Drizzle any remaining sauce from the skillet over the top.

6. Garnish with optional toppings such as chopped green onions, sesame seeds, or lime wedges, and serve immediately.

Nutritional values: Calories: 420 kcal, Protein: 30 g, Carbohydrates: 53 g, Sugars: 8 g, Fiber: 4 g, Fat: 8 g, Saturated Fat: 1 g, Unsaturated Fat: 7 g, Cholesterol: 215 mg, Sodium: 850 mg

BBQ PULLED PORK RICE BOWL

 PREP TIME: 15 MINUTES   **SERVINGS: 4**   **COOK TIME: 40 MINUTES (FOR PRE-COOKED PULLED PORK)**

INGREDIENTS:

- 2 cups white or brown rice
- 4 cups water
- 1 lb cooked pulled pork (store-bought or homemade)
- 1 cup BBQ sauce
- 1 15-oz can of black beans, rinsed and drained
- 1 cup frozen corn, thawed
- 1 avocado, sliced
- 1/2 cup chopped fresh cilantro
- 1/4 cup thinly sliced red onion
- Salt and pepper, to taste

DIRECTIONS:

1. In a medium saucepan, combine rice and water. Bring to a boil, then reduce heat, cover, and let simmer until the rice is cooked, following package instructions for time (usually 15-20 minutes for white rice, 35-40 minutes for brown rice).
2. Combine the pulled pork and BBQ sauce in a separate saucepan over low heat. Heat until warmed through, stirring occasionally.
3. Assemble the rice bowls by dividing the cooked rice among four bowls. Top each bowl with an equal portion of the BBQ pulled pork, black beans, corn, avocado slices, cilantro, and red onion.
4. Season with salt and pepper to taste, and serve immediately.

Nutritional values: Calories: 760 kcal, Protein: 37 g, Carbohydrates: 106 g, Sugars: 25 g, Fiber: 10 g, Fat: 21 g, Saturated Fat: 5 g, Unsaturated Fat: 16 g, Cholesterol: 90 mg, Sodium: 1150 mg

GRAIN BOWLS

MEDITERRANEAN QUINOA BOWL

 PREP TIME: 20 MINUTES    **SERVINGS: 4**    **COOK TIME: 15 MINUTES**

INGREDIENTS:

- 1 cup uncooked quinoa
- 2 cups water or vegetable broth
- 1/2 tsp salt
- 1 cup cherry tomatoes, halved
- 1 cup cucumber, chopped
- 1/4 cup red onion, finely chopped
- 1/3 cup Kalamata olives, pitted and halved
- 1/2 cup crumbled feta cheese
- 2 tbsp chopped fresh parsley
- 1/4 cup extra virgin olive oil
- Juice of 1 lemon
- Salt and pepper, to taste

DIRECTIONS:

1. Rinse the quinoa under cold water in a fine-mesh strainer. In a medium saucepan, combine the rinsed quinoa, water or vegetable broth, and salt. Bring to a boil over medium-high heat, then reduce the heat to maintain a gentle simmer. Cook until the quinoa has absorbed all of the liquid, about 15 minutes. Remove from heat, cover, and let the quinoa rest for 5 minutes. Fluff with a fork and set aside to cool.

2. Combine the cherry tomatoes, cucumber, red onion, Kalamata olives, feta cheese, and parsley in a large bowl.

3. In a small bowl, whisk together the olive oil and lemon juice. Season with salt and pepper to taste.

4. Once the quinoa has cooled, add it to the large bowl with the vegetables and cheese. Drizzle the dressing over the top and gently toss to combine. Adjust the seasoning if necessary.

5. Divide the Mediterranean quinoa mixture among four bowls or airtight containers. Serve immediately or store in the refrigerator for up to 3 days.

Nutritional values: Calories: 420 kcal, Protein: 12 g, Carbohydrates: 40 g, Sugars: 4 g, Fiber: 5 g, Fat: 24 g, Saturated Fat: 6 g, Unsaturated Fat: 18 g, Cholesterol: 22 mg, Sodium: 650 mg

ROASTED VEGETABLE FARRO BOWL

 PREP TIME: 20 MINUTES    **SERVINGS: 4**    **COOK TIME: 40 MINUTES**

INGREDIENTS:

- 1 1/2 cups farro
- 3 cups vegetable broth or water
- 1 medium sweet potato, peeled and cubed
- 1 red bell pepper, cut into 1-inch pieces
- 1 small red onion, cut into wedges
- 2 cups broccoli florets
- 3 tbsp olive oil
- Salt and pepper, to taste
- 1/4 cup crumbled feta cheese
- 1/4 cup chopped fresh parsley
- Optional: lemon wedges for serving

DIRECTIONS:

1. Preheat the oven to 425°F (220°C). Line a baking sheet with parchment paper.

2. In a medium saucepan, combine the farro and vegetable broth (or water). Bring to a boil, reduce heat to low, cover, and simmer for 25-30 minutes until the farro is tender but still chewy. Drain any excess liquid and set aside.

3. Place the sweet potato, red bell pepper, red onion, and broccoli on the prepared baking sheet. Drizzle with olive oil and season with salt and pepper. Toss to coat the vegetables evenly.

4. Roast the vegetables in the preheated oven for 20-25 minutes, stirring occasionally, until they are tender and lightly browned.

5. To assemble the bowls, divide the cooked farro among four bowls. Top each bowl with an equal amount of roasted vegetables. Sprinkle with crumbled feta cheese and chopped parsley.

6. Serve with lemon wedges on the side, if desired, for a burst of brightness and flavor.

Nutritional values: Calories: 530 kcal, Protein: 15 g, Carbohydrates: 83 g, Sugars: 7 g, Fiber: 13 g, Fat: 17 g, Saturated Fat: 4 g, Unsaturated Fat: 13 g, Cholesterol: 15 mg, Sodium: 550 mg

SOUTHWEST BARLEY BOWL

 PREP TIME: 15 MINUTES    **SERVINGS: 4**    **COOK TIME: 40 MINUTES**

INGREDIENTS:

- 1 cup uncooked pearl barley
- 3 cups vegetable broth or water
- 1 tbsp olive oil
- 1 small onion, diced
- 1 can (15 oz) black beans, rinsed and drained
- 1 cup cherry tomatoes, halved
- 1 cup frozen corn, thawed
- 1 jalapeño pepper, seeded and minced
- 1/2 tsp ground cumin
- 1/2 tsp chili powder
- Salt and pepper, to taste
- 1/4 cup chopped fresh cilantro
- 1 lime, cut into wedges
- Optional toppings: avocado slices, crumbled feta or cotija cheese, sour cream, or hot sauce

DIRECTIONS:

1. In a medium saucepan, combine the pearl barley and vegetable broth (or water). Bring to a boil, then reduce heat to low and cover. Cook for 35-40 minutes or until barley is tender and liquid is absorbed. Fluff with a fork and set aside.

2. In a large skillet, heat the olive oil over medium heat. Add the diced onion and cook until softened about 5 minutes.

3. Stir in the black beans, cherry tomatoes, corn, jalapeño pepper, cumin, chili powder, salt, and pepper. Cook for another 5-7 minutes until heated through.

4. To assemble the barley bowls, divide the cooked barley among four bowls. Top with the vegetable and bean mixture, then sprinkle with chopped cilantro. Add any desired toppings, such as avocado slices, crumbled feta or cotija cheese, sour cream, or hot sauce.

5. Serve with lime wedges for squeezing over the bowls, and enjoy!

Nutritional values: Calories: 400 kcal, Protein: 12 g, Carbohydrates: 71 g, Sugars: 6 g, Fiber: 13 g,, Fat: 7 g, Saturated Fat: 1 g, Unsaturated Fat: 6 g,Cholesterol: 0 mg, Sodium: 580 mg

KALE, BEET, AND GOAT CHEESE GRAIN BOWL

 PREP TIME: 15 MINUTES   **SERVINGS: 4**   **COOK TIME: 30 MINUTES**

INGREDIENTS:

- 1 cup uncooked farro
- 3 cups water or vegetable broth
- 4 cups chopped kale, stems removed
- 1 tbsp olive oil
- 2 medium beets, peeled and diced
- 1/2 cup crumbled goat cheese
- 1/4 cup chopped walnuts, toasted
- Salt and pepper, to taste

For the dressing:
- 1/4 cup olive oil
- 2 tbsp apple cider vinegar
- 1 tbsp honey
- 1 tsp Dijon mustard
- Salt and pepper

DIRECTIONS:

1. In a medium saucepan, combine the farro and water (or vegetable broth). Bring to a boil, then reduce heat to low, cover, and simmer for 25-30 minutes or until farro is tender and liquid is absorbed. Fluff with a fork and set aside.

2. Meanwhile, preheat the oven to 400°F (200°C). Toss the diced beets with 1 tablespoon of olive oil and season with salt and pepper. Spread on a baking sheet and roast for 25-30 minutes or until tender, stirring occasionally. Allow beets to cool slightly.

3. Massage the chopped kale with a pinch of salt in a large bowl until it softens and turns a deeper green color, about 1-2 minutes.

4. To prepare the dressing, mix the olive oil, apple cider vinegar, honey, Dijon mustard, salt, and pepper in a small bowl.

5. To assemble the grain bowls, divide the cooked farro among four bowls. Top with the massaged kale, roasted beets, crumbled goat cheese, and toasted walnuts. Drizzle the dressing over each bowl and serve immediately.

Nutritional values: Calories: 520 kcal, Protein: 15 g, Carbohydrates: 60 g, Sugars: 9 g, Fiber: 11 g, Fat: 27 g, Saturated Fat: 6 g, Unsaturated Fat: 21 g, Cholesterol: 15 mg, Sodium: 340 mg

NOODLE BOWLS

THAI CURRY NOODLE BOWL

 PREP TIME: 15 MINUTES    **SERVINGS: 4**    **COOK TIME: 20 MINUTES**

INGREDIENTS:

- 8 oz rice noodles
- 1 tbsp vegetable oil
- 1 small onion, thinly sliced
- 2 cloves garlic, minced
- 1 tbsp grated fresh ginger
- 2 tbsp Thai red curry paste
- 1 can (13.5 oz) coconut milk
- 3 cups vegetable broth
- 1 tbsp soy sauce
- 1 tbsp brown sugar
- 2 cups chopped mixed vegetables (such as bell peppers, carrots, snap peas, or baby corn)
- 1 cup cubed tofu, drained and pressed
- Juice of 1 lime
- 1/4 cup chopped fresh cilantro
- Optional toppings: sliced green onions, bean sprouts, chopped peanuts, or lime wedges

DIRECTIONS:

1. Cook rice noodles according to package instructions. Drain, rinse with cold water, and set aside.
2. Heat the vegetable oil over medium heat in a large pot or Dutch oven. Add the sliced onion and cook until softened about 5 minutes. Stir in the minced garlic and grated ginger, and cook for 1 minute.
3. Add the Thai red curry paste and cook, constantly stirring, for one more minute.
4. Pour in the coconut milk, vegetable broth, soy sauce, and brown sugar, and stir to combine. Bring the mixture to a simmer, then add the chopped mixed vegetables and cubed tofu.
5. Simmer for 10-12 minutes or until the vegetables are tender.
6. Remove from heat and stir in the lime juice and chopped cilantro.
7. To serve, divide the cooked rice noodles among four bowls. Ladle the Thai curry mixture over the noodles, making sure to include plenty of vegetables and tofu.
8. Garnish with optional toppings, such as sliced green onions, bean sprouts, chopped peanuts, or lime wedges.

Nutritional values: Calories: 560 kcal, Protein: 13 g, Carbohydrates: 66 g, Sugars: 9 g, Fiber: 5 g, Fat: 28 g, Saturated Fat: 20 g, Unsaturated Fat: 8 g, Sodium: 1000 mg

CHICKEN AND VEGGIE RAMEN BOWL

 PREP TIME: 15 MINUTES  **SERVINGS: 4**  **COOK TIME: 25 MINUTES**

INGREDIENTS:

- 4 packs (3 oz each) of ramen noodles, seasoning packets discarded
- 1 tbsp vegetable oil
- 1 small onion, thinly sliced
- 2 cloves garlic, minced
- 1 tbsp grated fresh ginger
- 6 cups chicken broth
- 2 cups shredded cooked chicken (rotisserie chicken works great)
- 2 cups chopped mixed vegetables (such as bok choy, mushrooms, and carrots)
- 2 tbsp soy sauce
- 1 tbsp mirin or rice vinegar
- Salt and pepper, to taste
- Optional toppings: sliced green onions, soft-boiled eggs, sesame seeds, or sriracha sauce

DIRECTIONS:

1. Cook ramen noodles according to package instructions without adding the seasoning packets. Drain, rinse with cold water, and set aside.
2. Heat the vegetable oil over medium heat in a large pot or Dutch oven. Add the sliced onion and cook until softened about 5 minutes. Stir in the minced garlic and grated ginger, and cook for 1 minute.
3. Pour in the chicken broth and bring the mixture to a simmer. Add the shredded cooked chicken and chopped mixed vegetables.
4. Simmer for 10-12 minutes or until the vegetables are tender.
5. Stir in the soy sauce and mirin (or rice vinegar). Taste and adjust seasoning with salt and pepper, if needed.
6. To serve, divide the cooked ramen noodles among four bowls. Ladle the chicken and vegetable broth over the noodles, including plenty of chicken and veggies.
7. Garnish with optional toppings, such as sliced green onions, soft-boiled eggs, sesame seeds, or sriracha sauce.

Nutritional values: Calories: 470 kcal, Protein: 28 g, Carbohydrates: 52 g, Sugars: 4 g, Fiber: 3 g, Fat: 16 g, Saturated Fat: 5 g, Unsaturated Fat: 11 g, Cholesterol: 60 mg, Sodium: 1450 mg

VIETNAMESE PHO NOODLE BOWL

 PREP TIME: 20 MINUTES    **SERVINGS: 4**    **COOK TIME: 30 MINUTES**

INGREDIENTS:

- 8 oz rice noodles
- 1 tbsp vegetable oil
- 1 small onion, thinly sliced
- 3 cloves garlic, minced
- 1 tbsp grated fresh ginger
- 8 cups beef broth
- 2 star anise
- 1 cinnamon stick
- 3 tbsp fish sauce
- 1 tbsp brown sugar
- 1 lb thinly sliced beef (such as sirloin, tenderloin, or flank steak)
- 4 cups bean sprouts
- 2 cups thinly sliced napa cabbage
- 1/4 cup chopped fresh cilantro
- Optional toppings: sliced jalapeños, Thai basil leaves, lime wedges, or sriracha sauce

DIRECTIONS:

1. Cook rice noodles according to package instructions. Drain, rinse with cold water, and set aside.

2. In a large pot or Dutch oven, heat the vegetable oil over medium heat. Add the sliced onion and cook until softened about 5 minutes. Stir in the minced garlic and grated ginger, and cook for 1 minute.

3. Pour in the beef broth and add the star anise, cinnamon stick, fish sauce, and brown sugar. Bring the mixture to a boil, then reduce the heat to low and let it simmer for 20 minutes.

4. Use a slotted spoon to remove the star anise and cinnamon stick from the broth.

5. To serve, divide the cooked rice noodles among four bowls. Arrange the thinly sliced beef, bean sprouts, and napa cabbage on top of the noodles.

6. Ladle the hot broth over the ingredients in each bowl, pouring it directly on the beef to cook it. The beef should be thinly sliced enough that the hot broth will cook it through quickly.

7. Garnish with chopped cilantro and optional toppings, such as sliced jalapeños, Thai basil leaves, lime wedges, or sriracha sauce.

Nutritional values: Calories: 580 kcal , Protein: 35 g, Carbohydrates: 71 g, Sugars: 7 g, Fiber: 4 g, Fat: 17 g, Saturated Fat: 5 g, Unsaturated Fat: 12 g, Cholesterol: 80 mg, Sodium: 1700 mg

SPICY MISO RAMEN BOWL

 PREP TIME: 15 MINUTES    **SERVINGS: 4**    **COOK TIME: 25 MINUTES**

INGREDIENTS:

- 4 packs (3 oz each) of ramen noodles, seasoning packets discarded
- 1 tbsp vegetable oil
- 1 small onion, thinly sliced
- 2 cloves garlic, minced
- 1 tbsp grated fresh ginger
- 6 cups vegetable broth
- 1/4 cup white miso paste
- 1/4 cup soy sauce
- 1 tbsp mirin or rice vinegar
- 1-2 tsp sriracha sauce, or to taste
- 2 cups chopped mixed vegetables (such as bok choy, mushrooms, and carrots)
- 1 cup cubed tofu, drained and pressed
- Optional toppings: sliced green onions, bean sprouts, nori sheets, or sesame seeds

DIRECTIONS:

1. Cook ramen noodles according to package instructions without adding the seasoning packets. Drain, rinse with cold water, and set aside.
2. In a large pot or Dutch oven, heat the vegetable oil over medium heat. Add the sliced onion and cook until softened about 5 minutes. Stir in the minced garlic and grated ginger, and cook for 1 minute.
3. Pour in the vegetable broth and bring the mixture to a simmer. In a small bowl, whisk together the white miso paste with a few tablespoons of the hot broth to make a smooth slurry. Stir the miso slurry into the simmering broth.
4. Add the soy sauce, mirin (or rice vinegar), and sriracha sauce to taste. Adjust the heat level to your preference.
5. Add the chopped mixed vegetables and cubed tofu to the pot, and simmer for 10-12 minutes or until the vegetables are tender.
6. To serve, divide the cooked ramen noodles among four bowls. Ladle the spicy miso broth over the noodles, including plenty of vegetables and tofu.
7. Garnish with optional toppings, such as sliced green onions, bean sprouts, nori sheets, or sesame seeds.

Nutritional values: Calories: 480 kcal, Protein: 15 g, Carbohydrates: 62 g, Sugars: 7 g, Fiber: 4 g, Fat: 18 g, Saturated Fat: 5 g, Unsaturated Fat: 13 g, Sodium: 2400 mg

TORTILLA TIME

QUESADILLAS

 PREP TIME: 10 MINUTES   **SERVINGS: 4**   **COOK TIME: 15 MINUTES**

INGREDIENTS:

- 1 pound boneless, skinless chicken breast, cooked and shredded
- 2 cups shredded cheddar cheese
- 1/2 cup diced red onion
- 1/2 cup diced bell pepper
- 1/4 cup chopped fresh cilantro
- 1 teaspoon ground cumin
- 1/2 teaspoon chili powder
- 8 flour tortillas
- 2 tablespoons olive oil

DIRECTIONS:

1. In a large bowl, combine the shredded chicken, cheese, red onion, bell pepper, cilantro, cumin, and chili powder. Mix well.

2. Heat a large skillet over medium heat. Brush one side of each tortilla with olive oil.

3. Place one tortilla in the skillet, oiled side down. Spoon some of the chicken mixture onto the tortilla, spreading it out evenly. Top with another tortilla, oiled side up.

4. Cook the quesadilla for 2-3 minutes or until the cheese is melted and the tortilla is golden brown. Flip the quesadilla and cook for an additional 2-3 minutes on the other side.

5. Repeat with the remaining tortillas and chicken mixture.

6. Slice each quesadilla into four wedges and serve hot.

Nutritional values: Calories: 564, Fat: 28g, Saturated Fat: 12g, Cholesterol: 135mg, Sodium: 780mg, Carbohydrates: 34g, Fiber: 3g, Sugar: 2g, Protein: 43g

BEAN AND CHEESE BURRITO

 PREP TIME: 10 MINUTES　　 **SERVINGS: 2**　　 **COOK TIME: 5 MINUTES**

INGREDIENTS:

- 1 cup canned refried beans
- 1 cup shredded cheddar cheese
- 1/4 cup chopped fresh cilantro (optional)
- 1/2 cup diced tomatoes
- 1/4 cup diced onion
- 2 large flour tortillas
- 1 tablespoon vegetable oil
- Hot sauce or salsa (optional)

DIRECTIONS:

1. Heat the refried beans over low heat in a small saucepan, occasionally stirring, until warmed through.
2. In a separate pan, heat the oil over medium heat. Add the onions and cook until softened about 3-4 minutes.
3. Warm the tortillas in a microwave for 15-20 seconds or in a dry skillet over low heat for 30 seconds on each side.
4. Assemble the burritos by spreading half of the beans in the center of each tortilla, followed by half of the cheese, tomatoes, onions, and cilantro. Add hot sauce or salsa if desired.
5. Fold the sides of the tortilla inwards and then roll up the burrito, tucking the bottom edge under the filling as you go.
6. Serve immediately with extra hot sauce or salsa on the side.

Nutritional values: Calories: 550, Fat: 28g, Carbohydrates: 55g, Fiber: 7g, Protein: 21g

TACO SALAD BOWLS

 PREP TIME: 20 MINUTES   **SERVINGS: 4 BOWLS**   **COOK TIME: 10 MINUTES**

INGREDIENTS:

- 4 large flour tortillas
- 1 tablespoon olive oil
- 1 pound ground beef or chicken
- 1 packet taco seasoning (1 ounce)
- 1/4 cup water
- 4 cups chopped romaine lettuce
- 1 cup cherry tomatoes, halved
- 1 cup shredded cheddar cheese
- 1 avocado, diced
- 1/2 cup black olives, sliced
- 1/4 cup red onion, finely chopped
- 1/2 cup sour cream or Greek yogurt for topping
- 1/2 cup salsa for topping

DIRECTIONS:

1. Preheat your oven to 375°F (190°C).
2. Warm the tortillas in the oven for 1-2 minutes, or until they are soft and pliable.
3. Brush each tortilla with olive oil on both sides.
4. Using an oven-safe bowl or a tortilla bowl mold, shape the tortillas into bowl forms, pressing them gently into the bowl or mold. Place them on a baking sheet.
5. Bake the tortilla bowls for 10-12 minutes or until they are crispy and hold their shape. Remove from the oven and let them cool.
6. While the tortilla bowls are baking, cook the ground beef or chicken in a skillet over medium heat until browned, breaking it apart as it cooks.
7. Add the taco seasoning and water to the skillet, stirring until the meat is well-coated with the seasoning. Cook for 3-4 minutes or until the liquid has mostly evaporated. Set aside.
8. Assemble the taco salad bowls by dividing the romaine lettuce among the tortilla bowls, then topping them with the cooked taco meat, cherry tomatoes, shredded cheddar cheese, avocado, black olives, and red onion.
9. Top each salad with a dollop of sour cream or Greek yogurt and a spoonful of salsa.

Nutritional values: Calories: 680, Fat: 42g, Saturated Fat: 14g, Carbohydrates: 43g, Fiber: 6g, Protein: 35g, Cholesterol: 100mg, Sodium: 800mg, Sugar: 5g

DINNER – EASY & TASTY RECIPES FOR BUSY STUDENTS

Now it's time to talk about the most satisfying meal of the day - dinner! I remember my college days when my friends and I would gather around a table full of tasty homemade dishes, sharing stories and laughter before diving into those long nights spent studying for exams. Ah, those were the days! But don't worry; we're going to explore some mouthwatering dinner choices that are just perfect for fueling your mind and body after a long day of classes and extracurriculars.

In this chapter, we'll focus on three key categories of dinner recipes that will make your life easier without sacrificing taste:

A. One-pot meals: Say goodbye to the dreaded mountain of dishes! We've got some fantastic pasta dishes, hearty stews and soups, and colorful stir-fries that'll leave you satisfied and ready to tackle that next study session. These recipes are perfect for busy students who want a good and nutritious meal without spending hours cleaning up afterward.

B. Sheet pan dinners: Incredible as it seems, you can make a whole meal on just one sheet pan! These recipes are perfect for whipping up in a hurry and make for easy cleanup. These dishes are healthy and flavorful, from baked chicken and veggies to roasted fish and greens. And let's not forget the crowd-pleasing sheet pan fajitas - perfect for those impromptu dinner parties with your college buddies.

C. Meatless options: Whether you're a full-time vegetarian or just looking to explore the veggies, these meatless options are perfect for adding some variety to your dinner routine. We've got some delicious vegetarian curries, satisfying veggie burgers, and delectable stuffed bell peppers that will keep you returning for more.

So let's dive into the realm of delicious and easy-to-make dinners that will nourish your body and delight your taste buds. Here's to memorable meals and long nights spent conquering those exams!

PART I

ONE-POT MEALS PASTA DISHES

CREAMY SPINACH AND MUSHROOM ALFREDO

 PREP TIME: 15 MINUTES    **SERVINGS: 4**    **COOK TIME: 20 MINUTES**

INGREDIENTS:

- 8 oz fettuccine pasta
- 2 tbsp unsalted butter
- 1 small onion, finely chopped
- 2 garlic cloves, minced
- 8 oz fresh mushrooms, sliced
- 2 cups fresh spinach, roughly chopped
- 1 cup heavy cream
- 1 cup grated Parmesan cheese
- Salt and pepper, to taste
- Optional garnish: chopped fresh parsley or basil

DIRECTIONS:

1. Cook the fettuccine pasta according to package instructions in a large pot of salted boiling water until al dente. Drain the pasta and set aside, reserving 1/2 cup of pasta water.

2. In a large skillet, melt the butter over medium heat. Add the onion and cook until softened about 3-4 minutes. Add the garlic and cook for an additional 1 minute until fragrant.

3. Add the sliced mushrooms to the skillet and cook until they release their moisture and start to brown, about 5-7 minutes. Stir in the chopped spinach and cook for 2-3 minutes, until wilted.

4. Pour the heavy cream into the skillet and bring the mixture to a simmer. Reduce the heat to low and gradually stir in the Parmesan cheese, allowing it to melt and create a creamy sauce. If the sauce is too thick, add the reserved pasta water, one tablespoon at a time, until the desired consistency is reached.

5. Add the cooked fettuccine to the skillet, tossing to combine with the sauce and vegetables. Season with salt and pepper to taste.

6. Serve immediately, garnishing with chopped fresh parsley or basil, if desired.

Nutritional values: Calories: 630 kcal, Protein: 23 g, Carbohydrates: 52 g, Sugars: 4 g, Fiber: 3 g, Fat: 37 g, Saturated Fat: 23 g, Unsaturated Fat: 14 g, Cholesterol: 120 mg, Sodium: 550 mg

ONE-POT CHILI MAC AND CHEESE

 PREP TIME: 15 MINUTES    **SERVINGS: 4**    **COOK TIME: 25 MINUTES**

INGREDIENTS:

- 2 cups elbow macaroni, uncooked
- 1 1/2 cups shredded cheddar cheese
- 1 tbsp olive oil
- 1 small onion, chopped
- 2 garlic cloves, minced
- 1 lb ground beef or turkey
- 1 can (14.5 oz) diced tomatoes, undrained
- 1 can (8 oz) tomato sauce
- 1 1/2 cups water
- 1 1/2 tsp chili powder
- 1 tsp ground cumin
- Salt and pepper, to taste
- Optional garnish: sliced green onions or chopped fresh cilantro

DIRECTIONS:

1. Heat the olive oil over medium heat in a large pot or deep skillet. Add the chopped onion and cook until softened about 3-4 minutes. Add the garlic and cook for an additional 1 minute until fragrant.

2. Add the ground beef or turkey to the pot, breaking it apart as it cooks. Cook until no longer pink, about 5-7 minutes. Drain any excess fat, if needed.

3. Stir in the diced tomatoes, tomato sauce, water, chili powder, cumin, salt, and pepper. Bring the mixture to a boil.

4. Add the elbow macaroni to the pot, stirring to combine. Reduce the heat to a simmer and cover the pot. Cook for 10-12 minutes or until the pasta is tender, occasionally stirring to prevent sticking.

5. Remove the pot from the heat and stir in the shredded cheddar cheese until melted and fully incorporated.

6. Serve immediately, garnishing with sliced green onions or chopped fresh cilantro, if desired.

Nutritional values: Calories: 660 kcal, Protein: 38 g, Carbohydrates: 58 g, Sugars: 6 g, Fiber: 4 g, Fat: 30 g, Saturated Fat: 13 g, Unsaturated Fat: 17 g, Cholesterol: 100 mg, Sodium: 850 mg

TOMATO BASIL PASTA WITH SAUSAGE

 PREP TIME: 15 MINUTES   **SERVINGS: 4**    **COOK TIME: 20 MINUTES**

INGREDIENTS:

- 8 oz linguine or spaghetti
- 1 tbsp olive oil
- 4 Italian sausages (about 1 lb), sliced into 1/2-inch thick rounds
- 1 small onion, chopped
- 2 garlic cloves, minced
- 1 can (14.5 oz) diced tomatoes, undrained
- 1/2 cup chicken broth
- 1/2 cup heavy cream
- 1/4 cup fresh basil, chopped
- Salt and pepper, to taste
- Grated Parmesan cheese for serving (optional)

DIRECTIONS:

1. Cook the linguine or spaghetti according to package instructions in a large pot of salted boiling water until al dente. Drain the pasta and set aside.

2. In a large skillet, heat the olive oil over medium heat. Add the sliced sausages and cook until browned and cooked through about 5-7 minutes. Remove the sausages from the skillet and set aside.

3. In the same skillet, add the chopped onion and cook until softened about 3-4 minutes. Add the garlic and cook for an additional 1 minute until fragrant.

4. Stir in the diced tomatoes and chicken broth, and bring the mixture to a boil. Reduce the heat to low and simmer for 5 minutes.

5. Add the heavy cream, cooked sausages, and chopped basil to the skillet, stirring to combine. Cook for 2-3 minutes until the sauce is heated. Season with salt and pepper to taste.

6. Serve the pasta topped with the sausage and tomato basil sauce, garnished with grated Parmesan cheese, if desired.

Nutritional values: Calories: 680 kcal, Protein: 28 g, Carbohydrates: 53 g, Sugars: 6 g, Fiber: 3 g, Fat: 39 g, Saturated Fat: 15 g, Unsaturated Fat: 24 g, Cholesterol: 85 mg, Sodium: 1050 mg

GARLIC SHRIMP AND ASPARAGUS LINGUINE

 PREP TIME: 15 MINUTES   **SERVINGS: 4**   **COOK TIME: 20 MINUTES**

INGREDIENTS:

- 12 oz linguine pasta
- 1 lb large shrimp, peeled and deveined
- 1 lb asparagus, trimmed and cut into 2-inch pieces
- 4 cloves garlic, minced
- 1/4 cup olive oil
- 1/4 cup dry white wine
- 1/2 cup chicken broth
- 1/4 cup grated Parmesan cheese
- Salt and black pepper to taste
- Fresh parsley, chopped for garnish

DIRECTIONS:

1. Cook linguine according to package instructions until al dente. Drain and set aside.
2. In a large skillet, heat olive oil over medium-high heat. Add minced garlic and sauté until fragrant, about 1 minute.
3. Add the asparagus to the skillet and cook for 5 minutes, stirring occasionally.
4. Add the shrimp to the skillet and cook until pink and cooked through about 3-4 minutes.
5. Pour in the white wine and chicken broth and let it simmer for 2-3 minutes until the liquid has reduced slightly.
6. Add the cooked linguine to the skillet and toss everything together to combine.
7. Sprinkle grated Parmesan cheese over the top and toss everything together again.
8. Season with salt and black pepper to taste.
9. Garnish with chopped fresh parsley and serve hot.

Nutritional values: Calories: 430, Fat: 18g, Saturated Fat: 3.5g, Cholesterol: 180mg, Sodium: 510mg, Carbohydrates: 38g, Fiber: 4g, Sugar: 3g, Protein: 28g

LEMON GARLIC BUTTER SPAGHETTI RECIPE

 PREP TIME: 10 MINUTES   **SERVINGS: 4**   **COOK TIME: 20 MINUTES**

INGREDIENTS:

- 8 oz spaghetti
- 3 tablespoons unsalted butter
- 3 cloves garlic, minced
- 1/4 cup freshly squeezed lemon juice
- 1/4 cup grated Parmesan cheese
- Salt and pepper to taste
- Chopped fresh parsley for garnish

DIRECTIONS:

1. Cook spaghetti in a large pot of boiling salted water according to package instructions until al dente. Reserve 1/2 cup of pasta water and drain the rest.

2. In a large skillet, melt the butter over medium heat. Add garlic and cook for 1-2 minutes until fragrant.

3. Add lemon juice to the skillet and stir well to combine. Let it simmer for 2-3 minutes until the liquid is reduced by half.

4. Add cooked spaghetti to the skillet and toss well to coat with the lemon garlic butter sauce. If the sauce is too thick, add some reserved pasta water to thin it out.

5. Add Parmesan cheese to the skillet and toss again to coat everything evenly.

6. Season with salt and pepper to taste. Garnish with chopped fresh parsley and serve hot.

Nutritional values: Calories: 274, Fat: 11g, Saturated Fat: 6g, Cholesterol: 25mg, Sodium: 139mg, Potassium: 146mg, Carbohydrates: 35g, Fiber: 2g, Sugar: 2g, Protein: 8g

STEWS
AND
SOUPS

HEARTY CHICKEN AND VEGETABLE STEW RECIPE

 PREP TIME: 20 MINUTES   **SERVINGS: 6**

INGREDIENTS:

- 1 lb boneless, skinless chicken breasts cut into bite-sized pieces
- 2 tbsp olive oil
- 1 onion, chopped
- 3 garlic cloves, minced
- 2 medium-sized carrots, sliced
- 2 celery stalks, sliced
- 2 cups chopped potatoes
- 2 cups chopped butternut squash
- 1 can (14.5 oz) diced tomatoes, undrained
- 3 cups low-sodium chicken broth
- 2 bay leaves
- 1 tsp dried thyme
- Salt and pepper, to taste
- Fresh parsley, chopped, for garnish (optional)

DIRECTIONS:

1. Heat olive oil over medium-high heat in a large pot or Dutch oven. Add the chicken pieces and cook for 5-7 minutes or until browned on all sides. Remove the chicken from the pot and set aside.
2. In the same pot, add onions and garlic and sauté for 2-3 minutes until softened.
3. Add the sliced carrots and celery and cook for 5-7 minutes until they soften.
4. Add the chopped potatoes and butternut squash to the pot and stir well.
5. Pour in the undrained diced tomatoes and chicken broth.
6. Add the bay leaves, thyme, salt, and pepper. Bring the mixture to a boil, then reduce the heat and let it simmer for 25-30 minutes or until the vegetables are tender.
7. Stir in the cooked chicken and let it simmer for an additional 10-15 minutes or until the chicken is heated through.
8. Remove the bay leaves and discard them.
9. Serve the stew hot, garnished with fresh parsley if desired.

Nutritional values: Calories: 268, Fat: 8g, Saturated Fat: 1g, Cholesterol: 48mg, Sodium: 295mg, Carbohydrates: 26g, Fiber: 5g, Sugar: 6g, Protein: 24g

BEEF AND BARLEY SOUP

 PREP TIME: 15 MINUTES   **SERVINGS: 6**   **COOK TIME: 1 HOUR 30 MINUTES**

INGREDIENTS:

- 1 pound stew beef, cut into bite-size pieces
- 1 cup pearl barley
- 1 onion, chopped
- 2 cloves garlic, minced
- 3 carrots, chopped
- 3 stalks of celery, chopped
- 8 cups beef broth
- 1 can of diced tomatoes
- 2 bay leaves
- 1 tsp dried thyme
- Salt and black pepper, to taste
- 2 tbsp olive oil

DIRECTIONS:

1. Heat the olive oil in a large pot over medium heat. Add the beef and cook until browned on all sides. Remove the beef from the pot and set aside.
2. Add the onion, garlic, carrots, and celery to the pot and sauté for 5 minutes or until softened.
3. Add the beef back to the pot along with the beef broth, barley, diced tomatoes, bay leaves, thyme, salt, and black pepper. Bring to a boil.
4. Reduce the heat to low, cover, and simmer for 1 hour or until the beef and barley are tender.
5. Remove the bay leaves and adjust the seasoning to taste. Serve hot.

Nutritional values: Calories: 320, Fat: 11g, Saturated Fat: 3g, Cholesterol: 65mg, Sodium: 1300mg, Carbohydrates: 29g, Fiber: 7g, Sugar: 4g, Protein: 26g

WHITE BEAN AND KALE MINESTRONE

 PREP TIME: 10 MINUTES   **SERVINGS: 6**    **COOK TIME: 30 MINUTES**

INGREDIENTS:

- 2 cans (15 oz each) of white beans, drained and rinsed
- 1 bunch of kale, stemmed and chopped
- 1 cup small pasta shells
- 2 tbsp olive oil
- 1 onion, diced
- 3 cloves garlic, minced
- 2 carrots, peeled and diced
- 2 stalks of celery, diced
- 1 tsp dried thyme
- 1 tsp dried oregano
- 1 tsp salt
- 1/2 tsp black pepper
- 1 can (14.5 oz) of diced tomatoes
- 4 cups vegetable broth
- 1/4 cup grated Parmesan cheese (optional)

DIRECTIONS:

1. Heat the olive oil in a large pot over medium heat. Add the onion and cook for 3-4 minutes, until soft.
2. Add the garlic, carrots, and celery, and cook for another 3-4 minutes until the vegetables are slightly softened.
3. Add the thyme, oregano, salt, and black pepper, and combine.
4. Add the diced tomatoes and vegetable broth, and bring the mixture to a boil.
5. Reduce the heat to low and add the white beans, kale, and pasta shells.
6. Simmer for 10-15 minutes until the pasta and kale are tender.
7. Serve hot, topped with grated Parmesan cheese if desired.

Nutritional values: Calories: 274, Fat: 7g, Saturated Fat: 1g, Sodium: 1143mg, Carbohydrates: 41g, Fiber: 10g, Sugar: 5g, Protein: 13g, Vitamin A: 146%, Vitamin C: 54%, Calcium: 18%, Iron: 22%

COCONUT CURRY LENTIL SOUP

 PREP TIME: 10 MINUTES    **SERVINGS: 6**    **COOK TIME: 30 MINUTES**

INGREDIENTS:

- 4 cups vegetable broth
- 1 (14-ounce) can of diced tomatoes
- 1 (14-ounce) can of full-fat coconut milk
- 1 tablespoon olive oil
- 1 onion, diced
- 3 garlic cloves, minced
- 1 tablespoon grated ginger
- 1 tablespoon curry powder
- 1 teaspoon cumin
- 1 teaspoon coriander
- 1 teaspoon paprika
- 1 cup dried red lentils
- Salt and pepper to taste
- Fresh cilantro, chopped, for serving

DIRECTIONS:

1. In a large pot, heat the olive oil over medium heat. Add the onion and cook until softened about 5 minutes.
2. Add the garlic and ginger and cook for 1 minute until fragrant.
3. Stir in the curry powder, cumin, coriander, and paprika, and cook for another minute.
4. Add the dried lentils and vegetable broth to the pot. Bring to a boil, then reduce heat to low, cover, and simmer for 20 minutes until the lentils are tender.
5. Stir in the diced tomatoes and coconut milk. Season with salt and pepper to taste.
6. Simmer for an additional 5-10 minutes until heated through. Serve hot, topped with fresh cilantro.

Nutritional values: Calories: 255, Fat: 13g, Saturated Fat: 8g, Cholesterol: 0mg, Sodium: 693mg, Potassium: 604mg, Carbohydrates: 27g, Fiber: 11g, Sugar: 5g, Protein: 10g

SPICY LENTIL AND SWEET POTATO SOUP

 PREP TIME: 10 MINUTES    **SERVINGS: 4**    **COOK TIME: 40 MINUTES**

INGREDIENTS:

- 1 large sweet potato, peeled and cubed
- 1 cup dried red lentils, rinsed and drained
- 4 cups vegetable or chicken broth
- 1 can (14 ounces) of diced tomatoes, undrained
- 1 tablespoon olive oil
- 1 large onion, diced
- 2 cloves garlic, minced
- 1 teaspoon ground cumin
- 1 teaspoon ground coriander
- 1 teaspoon smoked paprika
- 1/4 teaspoon cayenne pepper
- 1/4 cup chopped fresh cilantro
- Salt and pepper to taste
- Lime wedges for serving

DIRECTIONS:

1. In a large pot, heat the olive oil over medium heat. Add the onion and garlic and cook for 5 minutes or until softened.
2. Add the cumin, coriander, smoked paprika, and cayenne pepper to the pot and stir well to combine.
3. Add the sweet potato, lentils, broth, and diced tomatoes to the pot. Bring the mixture to a boil, then reduce the heat to low and simmer for 30-35 minutes or until the sweet potato and lentils are tender.
4. Remove the pot from the heat and stir in the chopped cilantro. Season with salt and pepper to taste.
5. Serve the soup hot, garnished with additional cilantro and lime wedges on the side.

Nutritional values: Calories: 206, Total Fat: 4g, Saturated Fat: 1g, Cholesterol: 0mg, Sodium: 513mg, Total Carbohydrates: 34g, Dietary Fiber: 10g, Sugars: 6g, Protein: 10g

STIR-FRIES

CHICKEN TERIYAKI STIR-FRY RECIPE

 PREP TIME: 15 MINUTES   **SERVINGS: 4**

INGREDIENTS:

- 1 lb boneless, skinless chicken breasts sliced into thin strips
- 2 tbsp vegetable oil
- 2 cups mixed vegetables (such as bell peppers, broccoli, and carrots), chopped
- 1/4 cup low-sodium soy sauce
- 2 tbsp honey
- 2 tbsp rice vinegar
- 1 tbsp cornstarch
- 1 tbsp water
- 2 cloves garlic, minced
- 1 tsp ginger, minced
- 1/4 tsp red pepper flakes (optional)
- 2 cups cooked brown rice for serving

DIRECTIONS:

1. In a small bowl, whisk together soy sauce, honey, rice vinegar, cornstarch, water, garlic, ginger, and red pepper flakes (if using). Set aside.

2. Heat one tablespoon of oil in a large skillet or wok over high heat. Add the sliced chicken and cook for 3-4 minutes or until browned and cooked through. Remove chicken from the skillet and set aside.

3. Add the remaining tablespoon of oil to the skillet. Add the mixed vegetables and stir-fry for 3-4 minutes or until they are crisp-tender.

4. Add the cooked chicken back to the skillet, then pour the teriyaki sauce over the top. Stir everything together and cook for another 1-2 minutes until the sauce thickens and everything is heated through.

5. Serve over cooked brown rice.

Nutritional values: Calories: 345, Fat: 10g, Saturated Fat: 2g, Cholesterol: 74mg, Sodium: 682mg, Carbohydrates: 34g, Fiber: 4g, Sugar: 11g, Protein: 29g

VEGGIE-PACKED QUINOA FRIED RICE

 PREP TIME: 15 MINUTES    **SERVINGS: 4**    **COOK TIME: 25 MINUTES**

INGREDIENTS:

- 2 eggs, lightly beaten
- 1/4 cup green onions, chopped
- 1 cup quinoa
- 2 cups water
- 1 tablespoon olive oil
- 1 onion, diced
- 2 cloves garlic, minced
- 2 cups mixed vegetables (carrots, peas, corn, broccoli, bell peppers, etc.), chopped
- 2 tablespoons soy sauce
- 1 teaspoon sesame oil
- 1 teaspoon sriracha sauce (optional)
- Salt and pepper, to taste

DIRECTIONS:

1. Rinse the quinoa in a fine mesh strainer and drain well.

2. In a medium saucepan, bring the water and quinoa to a boil. Reduce the heat, cover, and simmer for 15-20 minutes or until the water is absorbed and the quinoa is tender.

3. In a large skillet, heat the olive oil over medium heat. Add the onion and garlic and cook for 2-3 minutes until the onion is translucent.

4. Add the mixed vegetables and cook for 5-7 minutes until tender.

5. Add the cooked quinoa to the skillet with the vegetables and stir well to combine.

6. Whisk together the soy sauce, sesame oil, sriracha sauce (if using), salt, and pepper in a small bowl.

7. Pour the sauce over the quinoa and vegetables and stir well to coat.

8. Make a well in the center of the quinoa and vegetables, and pour the beaten eggs into the well. Scramble the eggs until cooked, and then stir them into the quinoa mixture.

9. Add the green onions and stir to combine. Serve hot, and enjoy!

Nutritional values: Calories: 271, Total Fat: 9g, Saturated Fat: 1g, Cholesterol: 93mg, Sodium: 560mg, Total Carbohydrate: 37g, Dietary Fiber: 6g, Sugar: 5g, Protein: 12g

SPICY BEEF AND BROCCOLI STIR-FRY

 PREP TIME: 15 MINUTES   **SERVINGS: 4**    **COOK TIME: 15 MINUTES**

INGREDIENTS:

- 1 pound flank steak, sliced into thin strips
- 1 head broccoli, cut into small florets
- 1 red bell pepper, sliced
- 1 tablespoon vegetable oil
- 2 cloves garlic, minced
- 1 tablespoon grated ginger
- 1/4 cup low-sodium soy sauce
- 2 tablespoons honey
- 2 teaspoons cornstarch
- 1/4 teaspoon red pepper flakes
- Salt and pepper, to taste
- Cooked rice for serving

DIRECTIONS:

1. Whisk together soy sauce, honey, cornstarch, and red pepper flakes in a small bowl. Set aside.
2. Heat the vegetable oil in a large skillet over medium-high heat. Add the sliced beef and stir-fry for 2-3 minutes or until browned. Remove from the skillet and set aside.
3. Add the broccoli florets and sliced bell pepper to the skillet and stir-fry for 3-4 minutes or until tender-crisp.
4. Add minced garlic and grated ginger to the skillet and stir-fry for 30 seconds.
5. Add the beef to the skillet and pour in the soy sauce mixture. Stir-fry for 1-2 minutes or until the sauce thickens and coats the beef and vegetables.
6. Season with salt and pepper to taste. Serve the spicy beef and broccoli stir-fry over cooked rice.

Nutritional values: Calories: 360, Fat: 12g, Saturated Fat: 4g, Cholesterol: 68mg, Sodium: 820mg, Carbohydrates: 31g, Fiber: 4g, Sugar: 16g, Protein: 33

SHRIMP AND PINEAPPLE STIR-FRY

 PREP TIME: 15 MINUTES    **SERVINGS: 4**    **COOK TIME: 15 MINUTES**

INGREDIENTS:

- 1 pound large shrimp, peeled and deveined
- 2 cups fresh pineapple chunks
- 1 red bell pepper, sliced
- 1 green bell pepper, sliced
- 1 small onion, sliced
- 3 cloves garlic, minced
- 1 teaspoon grated ginger
- 3 tablespoons soy sauce
- 2 tablespoons honey
- 1 tablespoon rice vinegar
- 1 tablespoon cornstarch
- 2 tablespoons vegetable oil
- Salt and pepper to taste
- Cooked rice for serving

DIRECTIONS:

1. Whisk together soy sauce, honey, rice vinegar, and cornstarch in a small bowl until smooth. Set aside.

2. In a large wok or skillet, heat vegetable oil over medium-high heat. Add garlic and ginger and cook for 30 seconds until fragrant.

3. Add sliced onions, red bell pepper, and green bell pepper to the skillet. Cook for 3-4 minutes, stirring occasionally, until vegetables are slightly softened.

4. Add shrimp to the skillet and cook for 2-3 minutes, until they turn pink and are cooked through.

5. Add pineapple chunks to the skillet and cook for another 2-3 minutes until they are slightly caramelized.

6. Pour the sauce over the shrimp and pineapple mixture and stir well to coat everything evenly. Cook for 1-2 minutes until the sauce has thickened.

7. Season with salt and pepper to taste. Serve hot with cooked rice.

Nutritional values: Calories: 304, Fat: 9g, Saturated Fat: 1g, Cholesterol: 214mg, Sodium: 1104mg, Potassium: 416mg, Carbohydrates: 26g, Fiber: 2g, Sugar: 18g, Protein: 29g

EASY VEGETABLE STIR-FRY WITH TOFU

 PREP TIME: 15 MINUTES   SERVINGS: 4

INGREDIENTS:

- 14 oz. extra-firm tofu drained and pressed
- 2 tbsp. soy sauce
- 1 tbsp. cornstarch
- 2 tbsp. vegetable oil, divided
- 1 red bell pepper, sliced
- 1 yellow bell pepper, sliced
- 1 small onion, sliced
- 2 cups broccoli florets
- 1 cup sliced mushrooms
- 3 cloves garlic, minced
- 1 tbsp. grated fresh ginger
- 2 tbsp. hoisin sauce
- 1 tbsp. rice vinegar
- 2 tbsp. water
- Salt and pepper, to taste
- Cooked rice or noodles for serving

DIRECTIONS:

1. Cut the pressed tofu into small cubes and toss with soy sauce and cornstarch until evenly coated.
2. Heat 1 tablespoon of vegetable oil in a large wok or skillet over medium-high heat. Add the tofu and cook until golden and crispy, about 5-7 minutes. Remove from the wok and set aside.
3. Heat the remaining tablespoon of vegetable oil over medium-high heat in the same wok. Add the bell peppers, onion, broccoli, and mushrooms, and cook until slightly softened about 5 minutes.
4. Add the garlic and ginger and stir for 1-2 minutes until fragrant.
5. Whisk together the hoisin sauce, rice vinegar, and water in a small bowl. Add the sauce to the wok and stir until the vegetables are coated.
6. Return the tofu to the wok and toss everything together until heated through.
7. Season with salt and pepper to taste. Serve the stir-fry over cooked rice or noodles.

Nutritional values: Calories: 243, Fat: 12.9g, Carbohydrates: 19.3g, Fiber: 5.5g, Protein: 14.9g

PART II

SHEET PAN DINNERS

-

BAKED CHICKEN AND VEGGIES

LEMON GARLIC CHICKEN AND ASPARAGUS SHEET PAN

 PREP TIME: 10 MINUTES    **SERVINGS: 4**   **COOK TIME: 20 MINUTES**

INGREDIENTS:

- 4 boneless, skinless chicken breasts
- 1 pound asparagus, ends trimmed
- 1 lemon, sliced
- 4 garlic cloves, minced
- 2 tablespoons olive oil
- 1 teaspoon dried thyme
- 1 teaspoon dried oregano
- Salt and pepper, to taste

Nutritional values: Calories: 269, Total Fat: 10g, Saturated Fat: 2g, Cholesterol: 97mg, Sodium: 208mg, Total Carbohydrate: 7g, Dietary Fiber: 3g, Sugar: 2g, Protein: 38g

DIRECTIONS:

1. Preheat the oven to 425°F, and line a sheet pan with parchment paper.
2. Arrange the chicken breasts in the center of the sheet pan.
3. Arrange the asparagus around the chicken.
4. Top the chicken with lemon slices and minced garlic.
5. Drizzle the olive oil over everything and sprinkle with thyme, oregano, salt, and pepper.
6. Bake for 20 minutes or until the chicken is cooked through and the asparagus is tender. Serve hot, and enjoy!

ONE-PAN CHICKEN THIGHS WITH ROASTED VEGETABLES

 PREP TIME: 10 MINUTES   **SERVINGS: 4**   **COOK TIME: 40 MINUTES**

INGREDIENTS:

- 4 bone-in, skin-on chicken thighs
- 1 pound baby potatoes, halved
- 1 red bell pepper, seeded and chopped
- 1 yellow bell pepper, seeded and chopped
- 1 small red onion, chopped
- 2 cloves of garlic, minced
- 2 tablespoons olive oil
- 1 teaspoon dried thyme
- 1 teaspoon dried rosemary
- Salt and black pepper, to taste
- Fresh parsley, chopped (optional)

DIRECTIONS:

1. Preheat oven to 400°F (200°C).
2. In a large bowl, combine the halved baby potatoes, bell peppers, chopped onion, minced garlic, olive oil, dried thyme, rosemary, salt, and black pepper. Toss well to coat.
3. Spread the vegetables on a large baking sheet in a single layer.
4. Season the chicken thighs with salt and black pepper on both sides. Then arrange the chicken thighs on top of the vegetables.
5. Bake in the preheated oven for 35-40 minutes, or until the chicken is cooked through and the vegetables are crispy and tender.
6. Remove from oven and let it rest for 5 minutes before serving. Garnish with chopped parsley (optional) and serve.

Nutritional values: Calories: 450, Fat: 26g, Saturated Fat: 6g, Cholesterol: 110mg, Sodium: 120mg, Potassium: 1070mg, Carbohydrates: 26g, Fiber: 4g, Sugar: 4g, Protein: 26g

BALSAMIC CHICKEN AND VEGETABLES SHEET PAN

 PREP TIME: 10 MINUTES   **SERVINGS: 4**   **COOK TIME: 25 MINUTES**

INGREDIENTS:

- 4 boneless, skinless chicken breasts
- 1 red bell pepper, seeded and sliced
- 1 yellow bell pepper, seeded and sliced
- 1 red onion, peeled and sliced
- 1 zucchini, sliced
- 1/2 cup cherry tomatoes
- 2 tablespoons olive oil
- 1 tablespoon balsamic vinegar
- 2 cloves garlic, minced
- 1 teaspoon dried oregano
- Salt and black pepper, to taste
- Fresh parsley, chopped (optional)

DIRECTIONS:

1. Preheat oven to 400°F (200°C).
2. Combine the sliced bell peppers, sliced onion, zucchini, and cherry tomatoes in a large bowl.
3. Add the olive oil, balsamic vinegar, minced garlic, dried oregano, salt, and black pepper. Toss well to coat.
4. Spread the vegetables on a large baking sheet in a single layer.
5. Season the chicken breasts with salt and black pepper on both sides.
6. Place the chicken breasts on top of the vegetables.
7. Bake in the preheated oven for 20-25 minutes or until the chicken is cooked through and the vegetables are tender.
8. Remove from oven and let it rest for 5 minutes before serving.
9. Garnish with chopped parsley (optional) and serve.

Nutritional values: Calories: 300, Fat: 11g, Saturated Fat: 2g, Cholesterol: 80mg, Sodium: 150mg, Potassium: 910mg, Carbohydrates: 14g, Fiber: 4g, Sugar: 7g, Protein: 36g

ROASTED FISH AND GREENS

SALMON WITH BROCCOLI AND POTATOES

 PREP TIME: 10 MINUTES   **SERVINGS: 4**   **COOK TIME: 25 MINUTES**

INGREDIENTS:

- 4 salmon fillets (about 6 oz each)
- 1 pound baby potatoes, halved
- 1 head broccoli, cut into florets
- 1 lemon, thinly sliced
- 2 tablespoons olive oil
- 2 cloves garlic, minced
- 1 teaspoon dried thyme
- Salt and black pepper, to taste
- Fresh parsley, chopped (optional)

DIRECTIONS:

1. Preheat oven to 400°F (200°C).
2. Combine the halved baby potatoes, broccoli florets, lemon slices, olive oil, minced garlic, dried thyme, salt, and black pepper in a large bowl. Toss well to coat.
3. Spread the vegetables on a large baking sheet in a single layer.
4. Season the salmon fillets with salt and black pepper on both sides.
5. Place the salmon fillets on top of the vegetables.
6. Bake in the preheated oven for 20-25 minutes or until the salmon is cooked through and the vegetables are tender.
7. Remove from oven and let it rest for 5 minutes before serving.
8. Garnish with chopped parsley (optional) and serve.

Nutritional values: Calories: 400, Fat: 19g, Saturated Fat: 3g, Cholesterol: 90mg, Sodium: 110mg, Potassium: 1350mg, Carbohydrates: 26g, Fiber: 5g, Sugar: 3g, Protein: 32g

LEMON HERB COD AND ZUCCHINI SHEET PAN

 PREP TIME: 10 MINUTES   **SERVINGS: 4**    **COOK TIME: 20 MINUTES**

INGREDIENTS:

- 4 cod fillets (about 6 oz each)
- 1 zucchini, sliced
- 1 yellow squash, sliced
- 1 red onion, peeled and sliced
- 1 lemon, thinly sliced
- 2 tablespoons olive oil
- 2 cloves garlic, minced
- 1 teaspoon dried thyme
- Salt and black pepper, to taste
- Fresh parsley, chopped (optional)

DIRECTIONS:

1. Preheat oven to 400°F (200°C).
2. In a large bowl, combine the sliced zucchini, yellow squash, red onion, lemon slices, olive oil, minced garlic, dried thyme, salt, and black pepper. Toss well to coat.
3. Spread the vegetables on a large baking sheet in a single layer.
4. Season the cod fillets with salt and black pepper on both sides.
5. Place the cod fillets on top of the vegetables.
6. Bake in the preheated oven for 15-20 minutes or until the cod is cooked through and the vegetables are tender.
7. Remove from oven and let it rest for 5 minutes before serving.
8. Garnish with chopped parsley (optional) and serve.

Nutritional values: Calories: 240, Fat: 9g, Saturated Fat: 1.5g, Cholesterol: 50mg, Sodium: 120mg, Potassium: 750mg, Carbohydrates: 14g, Fiber: 4g, Sugar: 6g, Protein: 27g

GARLIC BUTTER SHRIMP AND GREEN BEANS

 PREP TIME: 10 MINUTES   **SERVINGS: 4**    **COOK TIME: 20 MINUTES**

INGREDIENTS:

- 1 lb. raw shrimp, peeled and deveined
- 1 lb. green beans, trimmed
- 4 cloves garlic, minced
- 4 tablespoons unsalted butter, melted
- 2 tablespoons olive oil
- 1/4 teaspoon red pepper flakes (optional)
- Salt and black pepper, to taste
- Lemon wedges for serving

DIRECTIONS:

1. Preheat oven to 400°F (200°C).
2. In a large bowl, combine the green beans, minced garlic, melted butter, olive oil, red pepper flakes (if using), salt, and black pepper. Toss well to coat.
3. Spread the green beans on a large baking sheet in a single layer.
4. Bake in the preheated oven for 10 minutes.
5. Remove the baking sheet from the oven and add the shrimp to the baking sheet. Toss the shrimp with the green beans, ensuring they're coated in the garlic butter mixture.
6. Return the baking sheet to the oven and bake for an additional 8-10 minutes, or until the shrimp is cooked through and the green beans are tender.
7. Remove from oven and let it rest for 5 minutes before serving, then serve with lemon wedges on the side.

Nutritional values: Calories: 260, Fat: 18g, Saturated Fat: 7g, Cholesterol: 200mg, Sodium: 380mg, Potassium: 460mg, Carbohydrates: 8g, Fiber: 3g, Sugar: 3g, Protein: 19g

SHEET PAN FAJITAS

SHEET PAN CHICKEN FAJITAS

 PREP TIME: 10 MINUTES    SERVINGS: 4    COOK TIME: 25 MINUTES

INGREDIENTS:

- 1 lb. boneless, skinless chicken breasts sliced into strips
- 2 red bell peppers, seeded and sliced
- 1 green bell pepper, seeded and sliced
- 1 yellow onion, peeled and sliced
- 3 tablespoons olive oil
- 2 tablespoons taco seasoning
- Salt and black pepper, to taste
- Flour tortillas for serving
- Optional toppings: shredded cheese, sour cream, guacamole, salsa, chopped cilantro

DIRECTIONS:

1. Preheat oven to 400°F (200°C).
2. In a large bowl, combine the sliced chicken, sliced bell peppers, sliced onion, olive oil, taco seasoning, salt, and black pepper. Toss well to coat.
3. Spread the chicken and vegetables in a single layer on a large baking sheet.
4. Bake in the preheated oven for 20-25 minutes or until the chicken is cooked through and the vegetables are tender.
5. Remove from oven and let it rest for 5 minutes before serving.
6. Serve with warm flour tortillas and optional toppings, such as shredded cheese, sour cream, guacamole, salsa, and chopped cilantro.

Nutritional values: Calories: 290, Fat: 14g, Saturated Fat: 2.5g, Cholesterol: 80mg, Sodium: 460mg, Potassium: 570mg, Carbohydrates: 11g, Fiber: 3g, Sugar: 5g, Protein: 29g

STEAK FAJITAS SHEET PAN DINNER

 PREP TIME: 10 MINUTES   SERVINGS: 4   COOK TIME: 25 MINUTES

INGREDIENTS:

- 1 lb. flank steak, sliced into strips
- 2 red bell peppers, seeded and sliced
- 1 green bell pepper, seeded and sliced
- 1 yellow onion, peeled and sliced
- 3 tablespoons olive oil
- 2 tablespoons taco seasoning
- Salt and black pepper, to taste
- Flour tortillas for serving
- Optional toppings: shredded cheese, sour cream, guacamole, salsa, chopped cilantro

DIRECTIONS:

1. Preheat oven to 400°F (200°C).
2. In a large bowl, combine the sliced flank steak, sliced bell peppers, sliced onion, olive oil, taco seasoning, salt, and black pepper. Toss well to coat.
3. Spread the steak and vegetables in a single layer on a large baking sheet.
4. Bake in the preheated oven for 20-25 minutes or until the steak is cooked to your preferred doneness and the vegetables are tender.
5. Remove from oven and let it rest for 5 minutes before serving.
6. Serve with warm flour tortillas and optional toppings, such as shredded cheese, sour cream, guacamole, salsa, and chopped cilantro.

Nutritional values: Calories: 340, Fat: 19g, Saturated Fat: 5g, Cholesterol: 75mg, Sodium: 580mg, Potassium: 630mg, Carbohydrates: 15g, Fiber: 3g, Sugar: 5g, Protein: 27g

VEGAN FAJITAS WITH PORTOBELLO MUSHROOMS

 PREP TIME: 10 MINUTES    **SERVINGS: 4**    **COOK TIME: 25 MINUTES**

INGREDIENTS:

- 4 portobello mushroom caps, sliced
- 2 red bell peppers, seeded and sliced
- 1 green bell pepper, seeded and sliced
- 1 yellow onion, peeled and sliced
- 3 tablespoons olive oil
- 2 tablespoons taco seasoning
- Salt and black pepper, to taste
- Flour tortillas for serving
- Optional toppings: avocado, salsa, chopped cilantro

DIRECTIONS:

1. Preheat oven to 400°F (200°C).
2. In a large bowl, combine the sliced portobello mushrooms, sliced bell peppers, sliced onion, olive oil, taco seasoning, salt, and black pepper. Toss well to coat.
3. Spread the vegetables on a large baking sheet in a single layer.
4. Bake in the preheated oven for 20-25 minutes or until the vegetables are tender.
5. Remove from oven and let it rest for 5 minutes before serving.
6. Serve with warm flour tortillas and optional toppings, such as avocado, salsa, and chopped cilantro.

Nutritional values: Calories: 170, Fat: 10g, Saturated Fat: 1.5g, Cholesterol: 0mg, Sodium: 580mg, Potassium: 610mg, Carbohydrates: 19g, Fiber: 5g, Sugar: 6g, Protein: 4g

MEATLESS OPTIONS

-

VEGETARIAN CURRIES

CHICKPEA AND SPINACH CURRY

 PREP TIME: 10 MINUTES   SERVINGS: 4   COOK TIME: 20 MINUTES

INGREDIENTS:

- 1 can (15 oz) chickpeas, drained and rinsed
- 1 can (14 oz) diced tomatoes
- 1 tablespoon olive oil
- 1 onion, chopped
- 2 cloves garlic, minced
- 1 tablespoon fresh ginger, grated
- 1 tablespoon curry powder
- 1 teaspoon ground cumin
- 1/2 teaspoon ground coriander
- 1/2 teaspoon turmeric
- 1/4 teaspoon cayenne pepper
- 1/2 cup vegetable broth
- 4 cups fresh spinach leaves
- Salt and pepper, to taste
- Cooked rice for serving

DIRECTIONS:

1. Heat the olive oil over medium heat in a large saucepan or dutch oven. Add the onion and cook until softened.

2. Add the garlic and ginger and cook for another minute, stirring constantly.

3. Add the curry powder, cumin, coriander, turmeric, and cayenne pepper. Cook for another minute, stirring constantly.

4. Add the chickpeas, diced tomatoes (with their juices), and vegetable broth. Bring to a simmer and let cook for 10-15 minutes, until the sauce has thickened slightly.

5. Add the spinach and cook until wilted, about 2-3 minutes.

6. Season with salt and pepper, and serve hot with cooked rice.

Nutritional values: Calories: 174, Fat: 5g, Carbohydrates: 27g, Fiber: 9g, Protein: 8g, Sodium: 605mg

CAULIFLOWER AND POTATO CURRY

 PREP TIME: 10 MINUTES   SERVINGS: 4   COOK TIME: 25 MINUTES

INGREDIENTS:

- 1 head cauliflower, cut into florets
- 2 potatoes, peeled and cubed
- 1 can (14 oz) diced tomatoes
- 1 tablespoon olive oil
- 1 onion, chopped
- 2 cloves garlic, minced
- 1 tablespoon fresh ginger, grated
- 1 tablespoon curry powder
- 1 teaspoon ground cumin
- 1/2 teaspoon ground coriander
- 1/2 teaspoon turmeric
- 1/4 teaspoon cayenne pepper
- 1/2 cup vegetable broth
- Salt and pepper, to taste
- Fresh cilantro, for serving
- Cooked rice, for serving

DIRECTIONS:

1. In a large saucepan or dutch oven, heat the olive oil over medium heat. Add the onion and cook until softened about 5 minutes.

2. Add the garlic and ginger and cook for another minute, stirring constantly.

3. Add the curry powder, cumin, coriander, turmeric, and cayenne pepper. Cook for another minute, stirring constantly.

4. Add the cauliflower, potatoes, diced tomatoes (with their juices), and vegetable broth. Bring to a simmer and let cook for 15-20 minutes, until the vegetables are tender.

5. Season with salt and pepper, then serve hot with cooked rice and fresh cilantro.

Nutritional values: Calories: 120, Fat: 3g, Carbohydrates: 22g, Fiber: 6g, Protein: 4g, Sodium: 440mg

LENTIL AND COCONUT CURRY

 PREP TIME: 10 MINUTES   SERVINGS: 4    COOK TIME: 25 MINUTES

INGREDIENTS:

- 1 tablespoon olive oil
- 1 onion, chopped
- 2 cloves garlic, minced
- 1 tablespoon fresh ginger, grated
- 1 tablespoon curry powder
- 1 teaspoon ground cumin
- 1/2 teaspoon ground coriander
- 1/2 teaspoon turmeric
- 1/4 teaspoon cayenne pepper
- 1 cup dried red lentils, rinsed and drained
- 1 can (14 oz) coconut milk
- 1/2 cup vegetable broth
- 2 cups fresh spinach leaves
- Salt and pepper, to taste
- Cooked rice for serving

DIRECTIONS:

1. In a large saucepan or dutch oven, heat the olive oil over medium heat. Add the onion and cook until softened about 5 minutes.
2. Add the garlic and ginger and cook for another minute, stirring constantly.
3. Add the curry powder, cumin, coriander, turmeric, and cayenne pepper. Cook for another minute, stirring constantly.
4. Add the lentils, coconut milk, and vegetable broth. Bring to a boil and then reduce to a simmer. Cover and let cook for 15-20 minutes, until the lentils are tender.
5. Add the spinach and cook until wilted, about 2-3 minutes.
6. Season with salt and pepper to taste. Serve hot with cooked rice.

Nutritional values: Calories: 300, Fat: 18g, Carbohydrates: 25g, Fiber: 9g, Protein: 12g, Sodium: 360mg

VEGGIE BURGERS

BLACK BEAN AND QUINOA BURGER

 PREP TIME: 10 MINUTES    SERVINGS: 4    COOK TIME: 20 MINUTES

INGREDIENTS:

- 1 can (15 oz) black beans, drained and rinsed
- 1/2 cup cooked quinoa
- 1/4 cup breadcrumbs
- 1 egg
- 1/4 cup red onion, chopped
- 1 garlic clove, minced
- 1 teaspoon cumin
- 1 teaspoon chili powder
- Salt and pepper, to taste
- 4 burger buns
- Toppings of your choice (lettuce, tomato, avocado, etc.)

DIRECTIONS:

1. In a large mixing bowl, mash the black beans with a fork until they are mostly broken down.
2. Add the cooked quinoa, breadcrumbs, egg, red onion, garlic, cumin, chili powder, salt, and pepper. Mix everything until well combined.
3. Divide the mixture into four equal portions and shape it into patties.
4. Heat a large skillet over medium-high heat. Add a little oil, then add the patties to the skillet.
5. Cook for 4-5 minutes on each side until the burgers are browned and crispy.
6. Serve the burgers on buns with your favorite toppings.

Nutritional values: Calories: 278, Fat: 6g, Carbohydrates: 45g, Fiber: 12g, Protein: 14g, Sodium: 418mg

PORTOBELLO MUSHROOM BURGER

 PREP TIME: 10 MINUTES    **SERVINGS: 4**    **COOK TIME: 10 MINUTES**

INGREDIENTS:

- 4 large Portobello mushroom caps
- 2 tablespoons balsamic vinegar
- 2 tablespoons olive oil
- 1 teaspoon dried oregano
- Salt and pepper, to taste
- 4 burger buns
- Toppings of your choice (lettuce, tomato, onion, cheese, etc.)

DIRECTIONS:

1. Preheat the grill or grill pan to medium-high heat.
2. Clean the mushroom caps and remove the stems.
3. Whisk together the balsamic vinegar, olive oil, dried oregano, salt, and pepper in a small bowl.
4. Brush the mushroom caps with the balsamic mixture on both sides.
5. Place the mushrooms on the grill or grill pan, gill side down. Grill for 4-5 minutes.
6. Flip the mushrooms over and grill for another 4-5 minutes until they are tender and juicy.
7. Toast the burger buns on the grill for 1-2 minutes.
8. Assemble the burgers by placing the mushroom caps on the buns and adding your favorite toppings.

Nutritional values (without optional additions): Calories: 189, Fat: 9g, Carbohydrates: 22g, Fiber: 3g, Protein: 5g, Sodium: 162mg

SWEET POTATO AND BLACK BEAN BURGER

 PREP TIME: 15 MINUTES SERVINGS: 4 COOK TIME: 25 MINUTES

INGREDIENTS:

- 1 large sweet potato, peeled and grated
- 1 can (15 oz) black beans, drained and rinsed
- 1/4 cup breadcrumbs
- 1 egg
- 1/4 cup red onion, chopped
- 1 garlic clove, minced
- 1 teaspoon cumin
- 1/2 teaspoon smoked paprika
- Salt and pepper, to taste
- 4 burger buns
- Toppings of your choice (lettuce, tomato, onion, avocado, etc.)

DIRECTIONS:

1. Preheat oven to 375°F.
2. Combine the grated sweet potato, black beans, breadcrumbs, egg, red onion, garlic, cumin, smoked paprika, salt, and pepper in a large mixing bowl. Mix everything together until well combined.
3. Divide the mixture into 4 equal portions and shape it into patties.
4. Heat a large skillet over medium-high heat. Add a little oil, then add the patties to the skillet.
5. Cook for 4-5 minutes on each side until the burgers are browned and crispy.
6. Transfer the burgers to a baking sheet and bake in the oven for 10-15 minutes until they are cooked through.
7. Serve the burgers on buns with your favorite toppings.

Nutritional values (without optional additions): Calories: 267, Fat: 4g, Carbohydrates: 51g, Fiber: 11g, Protein: 11g, Sodium: 370mg

STUFFED BELL PEPPERS

MEXICAN-STYLE QUINOA STUFFED PEPPERS

 PREP TIME: 10 MINUTES   **SERVINGS: 4**   **COOK TIME: 40 MINUTES**

INGREDIENTS:

- 4 bell peppers (any color)
- 1 cup quinoa
- 1 can (15 oz) black beans, drained and rinsed
- 1 cup corn (fresh or frozen)
- 1/2 cup red onion, chopped
- 1 jalapeño, seeded and chopped
- 2 garlic cloves, minced
- 1 teaspoon cumin
- 1/2 teaspoon chili powder
- 1/4 teaspoon paprika
- Salt and pepper, to taste
- 1 cup shredded Mexican cheese blend
- 1/4 cup fresh cilantro, chopped
- Lime wedges for serving

DIRECTIONS:

1. Preheat oven to 375°F.
2. Cut off the tops of the bell peppers and remove the seeds and membranes.
3. In a large pot, cook the quinoa according to the package instructions.
4. Combine the cooked quinoa, black beans, corn, red onion, jalapeño, garlic, cumin, chili powder, paprika, salt, and pepper in a large mixing bowl. Mix everything together until well combined.
5. Stuff each bell pepper with the quinoa mixture and place them in a baking dish.
6. Top each pepper with shredded cheese. Cover the dish with foil and bake for 25-30 minutes.
7. Remove the foil and bake for another 10-15 minutes, until the cheese is melted and bubbly.
8. Garnish with fresh cilantro and serve with lime wedges.

Nutritional values: Calories: 385, Fat: 13g, Carbohydrates: 53g, Fiber: 12g, Protein: 19g, Sodium: 524mg

SPINACH AND FETA STUFFED PEPPERS

 PREP TIME: 15 MINUTES    SERVINGS: 4    COOK TIME: 40 MINUTES

INGREDIENTS:

- 4 bell peppers (any color)
- 1 cup cooked rice
- 1 cup chopped spinach
- 1/2 cup crumbled feta cheese
- 1/2 cup chopped red onion
- 2 garlic cloves, minced
- 2 tablespoons olive oil
- Salt and pepper, to taste
- Lemon wedges, for serving

DIRECTIONS:

1. Preheat oven to 375°F.
2. Cut off the tops of the bell peppers and remove the seeds and membranes.
3. Combine the cooked rice, chopped spinach, crumbled feta cheese, red onion, garlic, olive oil, salt, and pepper in a large mixing bowl. Mix everything together until well combined.
4. Stuff each bell pepper with the rice mixture and place them in a baking dish.
5. Cover the dish with foil and bake for 25-30 minutes.
6. Remove the foil and bake for another 10-15 minutes, until the peppers are tender and the filling is heated through.
7. Garnish with lemon wedges and serve.

Nutritional values: Calories: 226, Fat: 10g, Carbohydrates: 28g, Fiber: 4g, Protein: 7g, Sodium: 326mg

COUSCOUS AND VEGETABLE STUFFED PEPPERS

 PREP TIME: 15 MINUTES   **SERVINGS: 4**   **COOK TIME: 45 MINUTES**

INGREDIENTS:

- 4 bell peppers (any color)
- 1 cup couscous
- 1 zucchini, chopped
- 1 yellow squash, chopped
- 1 red bell pepper, chopped
- 1/2 red onion, chopped
- 2 garlic cloves, minced
- 2 tablespoons olive oil
- 1 teaspoon dried oregano
- Salt and pepper, to taste
- 1/4 cup crumbled goat cheese
- Fresh parsley, chopped, for serving

DIRECTIONS:

1. Preheat oven to 375°F.
2. Cut off the tops of the bell peppers and remove the seeds and membranes.
3. Combine the couscous in a large mixing bowl with 1 cup of boiling water. Cover the bowl and let it sit for 5 minutes.
4. In a large skillet, heat the olive oil over medium heat. Add the chopped zucchini, yellow squash, red bell pepper, red onion, garlic, dried oregano, salt, and pepper. Cook for 10-12 minutes, until the vegetables are tender.
5. Add the vegetable mixture to the couscous bowl and mix everything until well combined.
6. Stuff each bell pepper with the couscous mixture and place them in a baking dish.
7. Top each pepper with crumbled goat cheese.
8. Cover the dish with foil and bake for 25-30 minutes.
9. Remove the foil and bake for another 10-15 minutes, until the peppers are tender and the cheese is melted and bubbly.
10. Garnish with fresh parsley and serve.

Nutritional values: Calories: 292, Fat: 10g, Carbohydrates: 41g, Fiber: 7g, Protein: 10g, Sodium: 139mg

WHOLESOME SALADS

MEDITERRANEAN COUSCOUS SALAD

 PREP TIME: 15 MINUTES   **SERVINGS: 4-6**   **COOK TIME: 10 MINUTES**

INGREDIENTS:

- 1 1/2 cups couscous (uncooked)
- 1 3/4 cups water or vegetable broth
- 1/2 teaspoon salt
- 1/4 cup olive oil
- 2 tablespoons fresh lemon juice
- 1 teaspoon honey (or agave for a vegan option)
- 1/2 teaspoon ground cumin
- 1/4 teaspoon black pepper
- 1 cup cherry or grape tomatoes, halved
- 1 cup cucumber, diced
- 1/2 cup red onion, finely chopped
- 1/2 cup Kalamata olives, pitted and halved
- 1/2 cup feta cheese, crumbled (optional)
- 1/4 cup fresh parsley, chopped
- 1/4 cup fresh mint, chopped

DIRECTIONS:

1. In a medium saucepan, bring water or vegetable broth and salt to a boil. Stir in couscous, then cover and remove from heat. Let stand for 5 minutes, until liquid has been absorbed. Fluff couscous with a fork and let it cool.

2. In a small bowl, whisk together olive oil, lemon juice, honey (or agave), ground cumin, and black pepper to create the dressing.

3. In a large bowl, combine cooled couscous, halved tomatoes, diced cucumber, chopped red onion, Kalamata olives, crumbled feta cheese (if using), chopped parsley, and chopped mint.

4. Pour dressing over the couscous mixture and toss gently to combine. Taste and adjust seasoning if necessary.

5. Refrigerate for at least 30 minutes to allow the flavors to meld. Serve chilled or at room temperature.

Nutritional values: Calories: 389 kcal, Total Fat: 17 g, Saturated Fat: 4 g (if using feta cheese), Sodium: 589 mg, Potassium: 304 mg, Total Carbohydrate: 49 g, Dietary Fiber: 4 g, Sugars: 5 g, Protein: 10 g

BROCCOLI AND CAULIFLOWER SALAD

 PREP TIME: 15 MINUTES  SERVINGS: 6

INGREDIENTS:

- 4 cups fresh broccoli florets
- 4 cups fresh cauliflower florets
- 1/2 cup red onion, finely chopped
- 1/2 cup raisins or dried cranberries
- 1/2 cup sunflower seeds or chopped nuts (optional)
- 1/2 cup plain Greek yogurt or mayonnaise
- 1/4 cup apple cider vinegar or white wine vinegar
- 2 tablespoons honey or maple syrup
- 1/2 teaspoon salt
- 1/4 teaspoon black pepper

DIRECTIONS:

1. In a large bowl, combine broccoli florets, cauliflower florets, chopped red onion, raisins or dried cranberries, and sunflower seeds or chopped nuts (if using).

2. In a separate small bowl, whisk together Greek yogurt or mayonnaise, apple cider vinegar, honey or maple syrup, salt, and black pepper to create the dressing.

3. Pour dressing over the broccoli and cauliflower mixture and toss gently to combine, ensuring all ingredients are evenly coated.

4. Refrigerate for at least 30 minutes to allow the flavors to meld. Serve chilled or at room temperature.

Nutritional values: Calories: 190 kcal, Total Fat: 9 g, Saturated Fat: 1 g, Cholesterol: 3 mg (if using Greek yogurt), Sodium: 276 mg, Potassium: 631 mg, Total Carbohydrate: 24 g, Dietary Fiber: 4 g, Sugars: 15 g, Protein: 7 g

KALE AND QUINOA SUPERFOOD SALAD

 PREP TIME: 20 MINUTES   **SERVINGS: 4**   **COOK TIME: 20 MINUTES**

INGREDIENTS:

- 1 cup uncooked quinoa
- 2 cups water
- 1/2 teaspoon salt
- 4 cups kale, chopped and stems removed
- 1/2 cup dried cranberries or cherries
- 1/2 cup roasted almonds, chopped
- 1 medium avocado, diced
- 1/4 cup red onion, finely chopped
- 1/4 cup feta cheese, crumbled (optional)
- 1/4 cup extra virgin olive oil
- 2 tablespoons lemon juice
- 2 tablespoons honey or maple syrup
- 1/2 teaspoon Dijon mustard
- 1/4 teaspoon salt
- 1/4 teaspoon black pepper

DIRECTIONS:

1. In a medium saucepan, combine quinoa, water, and salt. Bring to a boil, then reduce heat to low, cover, and simmer for 15-20 minutes, or until the quinoa is cooked and water is absorbed. Fluff with a fork and let it cool.

2. In a large bowl, combine chopped kale, cooked quinoa, dried cranberries or cherries, chopped almonds, diced avocado, chopped red onion, and crumbled feta cheese (if using).

3. In a small bowl or jar, whisk or shake together olive oil, lemon juice, honey or maple syrup, Dijon mustard, salt, and black pepper to create the dressing.

4. Pour dressing over the kale and quinoa mixture and toss gently to combine, ensuring all ingredients are evenly coated.

5. Refrigerate for at least 30 minutes to allow the flavors to meld. Serve chilled or at room temperature.

Nutritional values: Calories: 487 kcal, Total Fat: 27 g, Saturated Fat: 4 g (if using feta cheese), Cholesterol: 8 mg (if using feta cheese), Sodium: 443 mg, Potassium: 815 mg, Total Carbohydrate: 53 g, Dietary Fiber: 8 g, Sugars: 20 g, Protein: 13 g

ROASTED SWEET POTATO AND ARUGULA SALAD

 PREP TIME: 15 MINUTES    SERVINGS: 4    COOK TIME: 30 MINUTES

INGREDIENTS:

- 2 medium sweet potatoes, peeled and cubed
- 2 tablespoons olive oil, divided
- 1/2 teaspoon salt
- 1/4 teaspoon black pepper
- 4 cups arugula, washed and dried
- 1/2 cup goat cheese, crumbled (optional)
- 1/4 cup red onion, thinly sliced
- 1/4 cup toasted pecans or walnuts, chopped
- 2 tablespoons balsamic vinegar
- 1 tablespoon honey or maple syrup
- 1/4 teaspoon Dijon mustard

DIRECTIONS:

1. Preheat the oven to 425°F (220°C). Line a baking sheet with parchment paper.
2. In a large bowl, toss the cubed sweet potatoes with one tablespoon of olive oil, salt, and black pepper. Spread the sweet potatoes evenly on the prepared baking sheet.
3. Roast the sweet potatoes in the preheated oven for 25-30 minutes, or until they are tender and lightly browned, occasionally stirring for even cooking.
4. In a large salad bowl, combine the arugula, roasted sweet potatoes, crumbled goat cheese (if using), thinly sliced red onion, and chopped pecans or walnuts.
5. In a small bowl, whisk together the remaining one tablespoon of olive oil, balsamic vinegar, honey or maple syrup, and Dijon mustard to create the dressing.
6. Pour dressing over the salad and toss gently to combine, ensuring all ingredients are evenly coated.
7. Serve immediately, or refrigerate for up to 1 hour before serving to allow the flavors to meld.

Nutritional values: Calories: 315 kcal, Total Fat: 21 g, Saturated Fat: 5 g (if using goat cheese), Cholesterol: 13 mg (if using goat cheese), Sodium: 420 mg, Potassium: 543 mg, Total Carbohydrate: 28 g, Dietary Fiber: 4 g, Sugars: 14 g, Protein: 7 g

SNACKS AND STUDY BREAK BITES

Welcome to another mouthwatering chapter of this cookbook. Let's admit it, we all have those moments when our stomachs start to rumble, and we need something to munch on while we hit the books. But why are these tasty treats so important, and how do they differ? Stick with me, and you'll find out!

First, let's talk about why snacks and study break bites are essential. Picture this scenario: it's late at night, and you're in the library with your best friend, cramming for that big exam. That's exactly what happened with my bestie, Sam, and me during our freshman year. We were pulling an all-nighter, and suddenly, we were hit with those hunger pangs.

Thankfully, we'd packed an arsenal of healthful and nutritious snacks to keep our brains functioning. Not only did these delicious treats prevent us from losing focus and falling prey to junk food, but they also helped us ace that exam! So, having a variety of healthy snacks on hand can be a game-changer when it comes to powering through your study sessions.

Now for the two sorts of recipes I've prepared for you in this chapter: Nutritious Snacks and Guilt-Free Sweet Treats. What's the difference? Let me just break it down for you.

Nutritious Snacks are those wholesome, energy-boosting bites that are perfect for satisfying your hunger without weighing you down. Consider veggie sticks with hummus, fruits, yogurt parfaits, or homemade granola bars. These options provide essential nutrients and energy to keep your brain functioning properly, helping you stay focused and sharp during long study sessions.

On the other hand, Guilt-Free Sweet Treats are for those times when your sweet tooth simply cannot be resisted. Like when Sam and I finished a particularly difficult chapter and needed a reward to lift our spirits. These recipes, such as energy balls, fruit-based desserts, and healthy cookies, allow you to indulge without feeling guilty. They're made with wholesome ingredients and are much lighter than typical desserts, so you can enjoy a little sweetness without risking your study progress or your healthy eating habits.

So, there you have it, fellow scholars! This chapter is all about finding that perfect balance between nutrition, energy, and satisfaction. Prepare to be wowed by an array of drool-worthy nibbles and study break bites that will make your taste buds sing while keeping your brain firing on all cylinders. Happy snacking, and may the power of good food be with you during those late-night study sessions!

NUTRITIOUS SNACKS

TRAIL MIX WITH NUTS AND DRIED FRUIT

 PREP TIME: 10 MINUTES **SERVINGS: 8**

INGREDIENTS:

- 1 cup unsalted almonds
- 1 cup unsalted cashews
- 1 cup unsalted peanuts
- 1 cup raisins
- 1 cup dried cranberries
- 1/2 cup dark chocolate chips or chunks

Optional additions:

- 1/2 cup unsweetened coconut flakes
- 1/2 cup sunflower seeds or pumpkin seeds
- 1/2 cup chopped dried apricots or other dried fruit of choice

DIRECTIONS:

1. Combine the almonds, cashews, peanuts, raisins, dried cranberries, and dark chocolate chips in a large mixing bowl.
2. Add any optional additions, such as coconut flakes, sunflower seeds, or other dried fruits, if desired.
3. Stir well to ensure an even distribution of the ingredients.
4. Store the trail mix in an airtight container or resealable plastic bags for easy snacking on the go.
5. Enjoy a handful as a quick and convenient snack whenever you need an energy boost.

Nutritional values (without optional additions): Calories: 450, Fat: 27g, Saturated Fat: 6g, Carbohydrates: 47g, Fiber: 6g, Protein: 12g, Sodium: 20mg, Sugar: 30g

VEGGIE STICKS AND HUMMUS

 PREP TIME: 10 MINUTES **SERVINGS: 4**

INGREDIENTS:

- 1 cup of your favorite store-bought or homemade hummus
- 1 medium carrot, peeled and cut into sticks
- 1 medium cucumber, cut into sticks
- 1 bell pepper (color of your choice), cut into strips
- 1 cup cherry tomatoes
- 1 cup sugar snap peas
- Optional: 1 cup broccoli florets or cauliflower florets

DIRECTIONS:

1. Arrange the veggie sticks (carrot, cucumber, bell pepper) and other veggies (cherry tomatoes, sugar snap peas, and optional broccoli or cauliflower florets) on a plate or platter.
2. Place the hummus in a small bowl and put it in the center of the veggie arrangement.
3. Dig in! Dip your veggie sticks and other veggies into the hummus and enjoy.

Nutritional values: Calories: 180 kcal Protein: 7g, Carbohydrates: 24g, Fiber: 6g, Fat: 8g, Saturated Fat: 1g, Sodium: 280mg, Potassium: 580mg, Vitamin A: 2800 IU, Vitamin C: 100mg, Calcium: 80mg, Iron: 2.5mg

FRUIT AND YOGURT PARFAITS

 PREP TIME: 10 MINUTES   **SERVINGS: 2**

INGREDIENTS:

· 1 cup plain or vanilla Greek yogurt
· 1 cup granola (choose your favorite kind, but be mindful of added sugar)
· 1 cup mixed fresh fruit (strawberries, blueberries, raspberries, etc.)
· Optional: honey, maple syrup, or agave nectar for added sweetness
· Optional: 2 teaspoons chia seeds or flaxseeds for an extra Nutritional boost

DIRECTIONS:

1. Start by washing and preparing your fruit. Slice strawberries, if using, and set aside with the rest of the fruit.

2. In two tall glasses or mason jars, begin layering the parfait ingredients. Start with a layer of yogurt at the bottom, then a layer of granola, and then a layer of fruit.

3. Repeat the layers until the glasses are full, finishing with a layer of fruit on top.

4. Drizzle honey, maple syrup, or agave nectar over the top layer for added sweetness if desired. You can also sprinkle chia seeds or flaxseeds for an extra Nutritional kick.

5. Serve immediately or cover and refrigerate for up to 4 hours.

Nutritional values: Calories: 350 kcal, Protein: 17 g, Carbohydrates: 50 g (sugar content may vary depending on the granola and fruit used), Fat: 10 g (may vary depending on the granola used), Fiber: 6 g, Sodium: 55 mg

GRANOLA BARS

 PREP TIME: 10 MINUTES   **SERVINGS: 12 BARS**   **COOK TIME: 25 MINUTES**

INGREDIENTS:

- 2 cups old-fashioned rolled oats
- 1 cup unsweetened shredded coconut
- 1/2 cup chopped almonds or other nuts of your choice
- 1/2 cup dried cranberries or other dried fruits
- 1/2 cup honey or maple syrup
- 1/4 cup unsalted butter, melted
- 1/4 cup light brown sugar, packed
- 1 tsp vanilla extract
- 1/2 tsp ground cinnamon
- 1/4 tsp salt

DIRECTIONS:

1. Preheat your oven to 325°F (160°C). Line a 9x9-inch (23x23 cm) baking pan with parchment paper, leaving some overhang for easy removal.
2. Combine rolled oats, shredded coconut, chopped almonds, and dried cranberries in a large mixing bowl.
3. In a separate small bowl, whisk together honey, melted butter, brown sugar, vanilla extract, ground cinnamon, and salt until smooth.
4. Pour the wet mixture over the dry ingredients, and mix well, ensuring all the ingredients are evenly coated.
5. Transfer the mixture to the prepared baking pan, and press down firmly to create an even layer.
6. Bake for 25-30 minutes or until the edges are golden brown. Remove from the oven and let the granola bars cool completely in the pan.
7. Once cooled, use the parchment paper overhang to lift the granola bars out of the pan. Cut into 12 even bars, and store in an airtight container at room temperature for up to 1 week.

Nutritional values: Calories: 250 kcal, Fat: 12 g, Saturated Fat: 6 g, Carbohydrates: 32 g, Fiber: 4 g, Sugar: 18 g, Protein: 4 g, Sodium: 75 mg

BAKED SWEET POTATO CHIPS

 PREP TIME: 15 MINUTES    **SERVINGS: 4**    **COOK TIME: 25 MINUTES**

INGREDIENTS:

- 2 large sweet potatoes, thinly sliced (about 1/8-inch thick)
- 2 tablespoons olive oil
- 1/2 teaspoon sea salt
- 1/4 teaspoon black pepper
- **Optional seasonings:** smoked paprika, garlic powder, or cinnamon

DIRECTIONS:

1. Preheat your oven to 400°F (200°C) and line two large baking sheets with parchment paper.
2. Toss the thinly sliced sweet potatoes in a large bowl with olive oil, ensuring that each slice is evenly coated.
3. Arrange the sweet potato slices in a single layer on the prepared baking sheets, making sure they don't overlap.
4. Sprinkle the slices with sea salt, black pepper, and any optional seasonings you choose.
5. Bake the sweet potato chips in the preheated oven for 10 minutes. Then, remove the baking sheets from the oven and carefully flip the chips using a spatula or tongs. Return the baking sheets to the oven and continue baking for an additional 10-15 minutes, or until the edges of the chips are golden and crispy.
6. Remove the baked sweet potato chips from the oven and let them cool on the baking sheets for about 5 minutes. This will allow the chips to crisp up even more.
7. Transfer the cooled chips to a bowl or plate and serve immediately for the best taste and texture.

Nutritional values: Calories: 170, Fat: 7g, Saturated Fat: 1g, Carbohydrates: 25g, Fiber: 4g, Protein: 2g, Cholesterol: 0mg, Sodium: 320mg, Sugar: 5g

GOLDEN MILK SNACK BITES

 PREP TIME: 10 MINUTES    **SERVINGS: 12 SNACK BITES**    **COOK TIME: 30 MINUTES**

INGREDIENTS:

- 1 cup rolled oats
- 1/2 cup almond butter (or any nut butter of your choice)
- 1/4 cup honey (or maple syrup for a vegan option)
- 1 teaspoon ground turmeric
- 1/2 teaspoon ground cinnamon

DIRECTIONS:

1. Combine the rolled oats, almond butter, honey, turmeric, and cinnamon in a large mixing bowl. Mix well until all ingredients are thoroughly combined and form a sticky mixture.

2. Line a baking sheet with parchment paper or a silicone mat.

3. Using your hands or a small cookie scoop, form the mixture into 12 equal-sized balls, placing them onto the prepared baking sheet.

4. Place the baking sheet in the refrigerator to chill and set the snack bites for at least 30 minutes.

5. Once chilled and firm, transfer the golden milk snack bites to an airtight container and store in the refrigerator for up to one week.

Nutritional values: Calories: 130, Total Fat: 7g, Saturated Fat: 0.5g, Cholesterol: 0mg, Sodium: 20mg, Total Carbohydrate: 16g, Dietary Fiber: 2g, Sugars: 8g, Protein: 4g

GUILT-FREE SWEET TREATS

ENERGY BALLS

 PREP TIME: 15 MINUTES   **SERVINGS: 12 BALLS**   **CHILLING TIME: 30 MINUTES**

INGREDIENTS:

- 1 cup rolled oats
- 1/2 cup peanut butter (or any nut butter of your choice)
- 1/3 cup honey or maple syrup
- 1/2 cup unsweetened shredded coconut
- 1/2 cup ground flaxseed
- 1/2 cup mini chocolate chips (optional)
- 1 tsp vanilla extract
- A pinch of salt

Nutritional values: Calories: 190 kcal, Carbohydrates: 22g, Protein: 5g, Fat: 10g (3g saturated fat), Fiber: 3g, Sugar: 11g,

DIRECTIONS:

1. In a large mixing bowl, combine the rolled oats, peanut butter, honey, or maple syrup, shredded coconut, ground flaxseed, mini chocolate chips (if using), vanilla extract, and a pinch of salt. Stir well until all the ingredients are thoroughly mixed.

2. Cover the bowl and place it in the refrigerator for about 30 minutes. This will make the mixture easier to handle.

3. After chilling, use clean hands or a cookie scoop to form the mixture into 1-inch balls. You should get around 12 energy balls from the mixture. If the mixture is too sticky, you can dampen your hands with a little water before rolling the balls.

4. Store the energy balls in an airtight container in the refrigerator for up to 2 weeks. Enjoy them as a quick and healthy snack during study breaks or whenever you need an energy boost.

APPLE SLICES WITH PEANUT BUTTER

 PREP TIME: 5 MINUTES   **SERVINGS: 2**

INGREDIENTS:

- 2 medium apples (such as Fuji, Gala, or Honeycrisp), cored and sliced
- 4 tablespoons peanut butter (smooth or crunchy, depending on your preference)
- **Optional toppings:** Chopped nuts (such as almonds, walnuts, or pecans), Mini chocolate chips, Coconut flakes, Granola

DIRECTIONS:

1. Wash and core the apples, then slice them into thin, even rounds or wedges.

2. Lay out the apple slices on a plate or serving tray.

3. Spoon one tablespoon of peanut butter onto each apple slice evenly.

4. If desired, sprinkle optional toppings over the peanut butter-covered apple slices for added flavor and texture.

5. Serve immediately, or cover and refrigerate for up to 2 hours before serving to enjoy chilled.

Nutritional values: Calories: 250, Fat: 16g, Saturated Fat: 3g, Carbohydrates: 25g, Fiber: 5g, Protein: 7g, Sodium: 150mg, Sugar: 19g

MIXED BERRY CRUMBLE

 PREP TIME: 15 MINUTES   **SERVINGS: 6**    **COOK TIME: 30 MINUTES**

INGREDIENTS:

- 4 cups mixed berries (fresh or frozen, such as strawberries, blueberries, raspberries, and blackberries)
- 1/4 cup granulated sugar
- 1 tablespoon cornstarch
- 1 teaspoon lemon juice
- 1 teaspoon vanilla extract
- 1 cup rolled oats
- 1/2 cup whole wheat flour
- 1/4 cup packed brown sugar
- 1/4 cup chopped nuts (such as almonds, walnuts, or pecans)
- 1/4 teaspoon salt
- 1/4 cup unsalted butter, melted

DIRECTIONS:

1. Preheat your oven to 375°F (190°C). Grease a 9-inch baking dish with non-stick spray or butter.
2. Combine the mixed berries, granulated sugar, cornstarch, lemon juice, and vanilla extract in a large mixing bowl. Toss gently to coat the berries evenly. Transfer the berry mixture to the prepared baking dish.
3. Mix the rolled oats, whole wheat flour, brown sugar, chopped nuts, and salt in a separate bowl. Add the melted butter and mix until everything is combined and crumbly.
4. Sprinkle the oat mixture evenly over the berries in the baking dish.
5. Bake for 30-35 minutes, or until the topping is golden brown and the fruit is bubbling around the edges.
6. Remove from the oven and let the crumble cool for 10 minutes before serving. Enjoy warmly or with a dollop of Greek yogurt or a scoop of your favorite frozen yogurt.

Nutritional values: Calories: 280, Fat: 12g , Cholesterol: 20mg, Sodium: 120mg, Carbohydrates: 41g , Fiber: 5g, , Sugars: 23g, Protein: 5g

FRUIT SALAD WITH HONEY-LIME DRESSING

 PREP TIME: 20 MINUTES  **SERVINGS: 6**  **CHILLING TIME: 1 HOUR**

INGREDIENTS:

- 2 cups strawberries, hulled and halved
- 1 cup blueberries
- 1 cup pineapple chunks
- 1 cup kiwi, peeled and sliced
- 1 cup seedless grapes, halved
- 1 cup mandarin oranges, drained
- 2 tablespoons honey
- 1 tablespoon fresh lime juice
- 1 teaspoon lime zest
- 1/4 teaspoon vanilla extract
- Fresh mint leaves for garnish (optional)

DIRECTIONS:

1. Combine strawberries, blueberries, pineapple, kiwi, grapes, and mandarin oranges in a large mixing bowl. Gently toss the fruit to mix.

2. In a small bowl, whisk together the honey, lime juice, lime zest, and vanilla extract until well combined.

3. Pour the honey-lime dressing over the fruit and toss gently to coat the fruit evenly.

4. Cover the fruit salad and refrigerate for at least 1 hour to allow the flavors to meld together.

5. Before serving, give the fruit salad a gentle stir. Garnish with fresh mint leaves if desired. Serve chilled, and enjoy!

Nutritional values: Calories: 120, Fat: 0.5g , Cholesterol: 0mg, Sodium: 5mg, Carbohydrates: 30g , Fiber: 3g, Sugars: 24g, Protein: 1g

QUICK AND EASY DESSERTS

Hello, fellow dessert fans! I understand how hectic college life can be, with endless papers, exams, and social activities to juggle. But it shouldn't mean foregoing the sweet delights that make life a little more joyful, right? So I've compiled a list of delectable dessert recipes that are ideal for busy students like you.

These quick and easy dishes involve few ingredients, time, and kitchen expertise while still delivering great flavor. So, we've got you covered whether you're in the mood for something chocolatey, fruity, or simply decadent. Dive into this chapter to learn how to satisfy your sweet desire without working up a sweat!

MUG CAKE

 PREP TIME: 5 MINUTES   **SERVINGS: 1**   **COOK TIME: 1-2 MINUTES**

INGREDIENTS:

- 4 tablespoons all-purpose flour
- 2 tablespoons unsweetened cocoa powder
- 3 tablespoons granulated sugar
- 1/8 teaspoon baking powder
- a pinch of salt
- 3 tablespoons milk
- 2 tablespoons vegetable oil
- 1/4 teaspoon pure vanilla extract
- **Optional toppings:** Whipped cream, Ice cream, Chocolate chips, Fresh fruit

DIRECTIONS:

1. Combine the flour, cocoa powder, sugar, baking powder, and salt in a microwave-safe mug. Mix well with a fork.
2. Add the milk, vegetable oil, and vanilla extract to the mug. Stir until the batter is smooth and no lumps remain.
3. Microwave the mug on high for 1 minute. Check the cake for doneness by inserting a toothpick or fork in the center. If it comes out clean, the cake is made. If not, continue microwaving in 15-second intervals until fully cooked.
4. Allow the mug cake to cool for a minute or two before adding your favorite toppings. Grab a spoon and dig in!

Nutritional values (without toppings): Calories: 580, Fat: 34g, Saturated Fat: 4g, Carbohydrates: 67g, Fiber: 4g, Protein: 7g, Cholesterol: 3mg, Sodium: 150mg, Sugar: 37g

OATMEAL BANANA COOKIES

 PREP TIME: 10 MINUTES   **SERVINGS: 12 COOKIES**   **COOK TIME: 15 MINUTES**

INGREDIENTS:

- 2 ripe bananas, mashed
- 1 1/2 cups rolled oats
- 1/2 cup unsweetened applesauce
- 1/4 cup almond butter (or any nut butter of your choice)
- 1/4 cup dark chocolate chips or raisins (optional)
- 1/4 cup chopped nuts (walnuts, almonds, or pecans – optional)
- 1 tsp vanilla extract
- 1/2 tsp cinnamon
- 1/4 tsp salt

DIRECTIONS:

1. Preheat your oven to 350°F (175°C) and line a baking sheet with parchment paper or a silicone baking mat.
2. Mix the mashed bananas, rolled oats, applesauce, almond butter, and vanilla extract in a large bowl until well combined.
3. Stir in the cinnamon and salt.
4. Fold in the dark chocolate chips, raisins, and chopped nuts.
5. Drop the cookie dough onto the prepared baking sheet using a tablespoon or a small ice cream scoop, spacing them about 2 inches apart.
6. Gently flatten the cookies with the back of a spoon or your fingers.
7. Bake for 15 minutes or until golden brown cookies are firm around the edges.
8. Allow the cookies to cool on the baking sheet for 5 minutes before transferring them to a wire rack to cool completely.

Nutritional values: Calories: 120, Fat: 6g, Saturated Fat: 1g, Carbohydrates: 15g, Fiber: 2g, Sugar: 5g, Protein: 3g

CHOCOLATE CHIP COOKIES

 PREP TIME: 15 MINUTES

 SERVINGS: 24 COOKIES

 **COOK TIME: 10-12 MINUTES**

INGREDIENTS:

- 1/2 cup (1 stick) unsalted butter, softened
- 1/2 cup granulated sugar
- 1/2 cup packed light brown sugar
- 1 large egg
- 1 teaspoon pure vanilla extract
- 1 1/2 cups all-purpose flour
- 1/2 teaspoon baking soda
- 1/2 teaspoon salt
- 1 cup semisweet chocolate chips

DIRECTIONS:

1. Preheat your oven to 350°F (180°C). Line two baking sheets with parchment paper or silicone baking mats.

2. In a large bowl, cream together the softened butter, granulated sugar, and brown sugar until light and fluffy.

3. Add the egg and vanilla extract, mixing until well combined.

4. Whisk together the flour, baking soda, and salt in a separate bowl. Gradually add the dry ingredients to the wet ingredients, mixing until just combined.

5. Fold in the chocolate chips.

6. Using a cookie scoop or spoon, drop rounded tablespoons of dough onto the prepared baking sheets, spacing the cookies about 2 inches apart.

7. Bake for 10-12 minutes, or until the edges are lightly golden. Allow the cookies to cool on the baking sheets for 5 minutes before transferring them to a wire rack to cool completely.

Nutritional values: Calories: 145, Fat: 7g, Saturated Fat: 4g, Carbohydrates: 20g, Fiber: 1g, Protein: 2g, Cholesterol: 18mg, Sodium: 85mg, Sugar: 12g

RICE KRISPIE TREATS

 PREP TIME: 5 MINUTES   **SERVINGS: 12 SQUARES**   **COOK TIME: 10 MINUTES**

INGREDIENTS:

- 6 cups Rice Krispies cereal
- 4 cups mini marshmallows
- 1/4 cup (1/2 stick) unsalted butter
- 1/2 teaspoon pure vanilla extract (optional)

DIRECTIONS:

1. Grease a 9x13-inch baking pan or line it with parchment paper.
2. In a large saucepan, melt the butter over low heat. Add the marshmallows and stir continuously until completely melted.
3. Remove the saucepan from heat and stir in the vanilla extract.
4. Add the Rice Krispies cereal to the marshmallow mixture, stirring until the cereal is evenly coated.
5. Press the mixture into the prepared baking pan, using a greased spatula or wax paper to press it down firmly and evenly.
6. Allow the Rice Krispie treats to cool for about 30 minutes, or until set.
7. Cut into 12 squares and serve. Store any leftovers in an airtight container.

Nutritional values: Calories: 160, Fat: 4g, Saturated Fat: 2g, Carbohydrates: 29g, Protein: 1g, Cholesterol: 10mg, Sodium: 105mg, Sugar: 13g

NO-BAKE CHEESECAKE

 PREP TIME: 20 MINUTES    **SERVINGS: 8**    **CHILLING TIME: 4 HOURS**

INGREDIENTS:

Crust:
- 1 1/2 cups graham cracker crumbs (about 12 full sheets)
- 1/4 cup granulated sugar
- 1/2 cup (1 stick) unsalted butter, melted

Filling:
- 16 oz (2 blocks) cream cheese, softened
- 1 cup powdered sugar
- 1 teaspoon pure vanilla extract
- 1 cup heavy whipping cream, cold

DIRECTIONS:

1. Combine the graham cracker crumbs, sugar, and melted butter in a medium bowl. Mix until the crumbs are evenly coated with the butter.

2. Press the crust mixture into the bottom of a 9-inch springform pan or a pie dish, ensuring it's firmly packed. Chill the crust in the refrigerator while preparing the filling.

3. In a large bowl, beat the softened cream cheese until smooth and creamy. Gradually add the powdered sugar and vanilla extract, continuing to beat until well combined.

4. Wash the cold heavy whipping cream in a separate bowl until stiff peaks form.

5. Gently fold the whipped cream into the cream cheese mixture until fully combined, taking care not to deflate the whipped cream.

6. Pour the filling over the chilled crust, smoothing the top with a spatula.

7. Refrigerate the cheesecake for at least 4 hours, or preferably overnight, until set.

8. Before serving, run a knife around the edge of the cheesecake to loosen it from the pan, then release the springform sides or carefully cut and serve from the pie dish.

Nutritional values: Calories: 530, Fat: 39g, Saturated Fat: 23g, Carbohydrates: 42g, Fiber: 1g, Protein: 6g, Cholesterol: 115mg, Sodium: 350mg, Sugar: 30g

BROWNIES

 PREP TIME: 15 MINUTES   **SERVINGS: 16 SQUARES**   **COOK TIME: 25-30 MINUTES**

INGREDIENTS:

- 1/2 cup (1 stick) unsalted butter
- 1 cup granulated sugar
- 2 large eggs
- 1 teaspoon pure vanilla extract
- 1/3 cup unsweetened cocoa powder
- 1/2 cup all-purpose flour
- 1/4 teaspoon salt
- 1/4 teaspoon baking powder

Optional Add-ins:
- 1/2 cup chopped nuts (walnuts, pecans, etc.)
- 1/2 cup chocolate chips

DIRECTIONS:

1. Preheat your oven to 350°F (175°C). Grease a 9x9-inch baking pan or line it with parchment paper.

2. In a microwave-safe bowl, melt the butter. Allow it to cool slightly before adding the sugar, eggs, and vanilla extract. Mix well.

3. Whisk together the cocoa powder, flour, salt, and baking powder in a separate bowl. Gradually add the dry and wet ingredients, mixing until just combined.

4. If using, fold in the chopped nuts and/or chocolate chips.

5. Pour the batter into the prepared baking pan, spreading it evenly with a spatula.

6. Bake for 25-30 minutes, or until a toothpick inserted into the center comes out with a few moist crumbs. Be careful not to overbake.

7. Allow the brownies to cool in the pan for about 10 minutes before cutting them into 16 squares. Serve warm or at room temperature.

Nutritional values (per square, without add-ins): Calories: 130, Fat: 6g, Saturated Fat: 3.5g, Carbohydrates: 19g, Fiber: 1g, Protein: 2g, Cholesterol: 35mg, Sodium: 45mg, Sugar: 14g

CARROT CAKE QUINOA COOKIES

 PREP TIME: 15 MINUTES   **SERVINGS: 12 COOKIES**   **COOK TIME: 25 MINUTES**

INGREDIENTS:

- 1 cup cooked quinoa
- 1 cup rolled oats
- 1/2 cup grated carrots (about 2 medium carrots)
- 1/4 cup unsweetened applesauce
- 1/4 cup honey or maple syrup
- 1/4 cup raisins or chopped dates
- 1/4 cup chopped walnuts
- 1 teaspoon ground cinnamon
- 1/2 teaspoon ground nutmeg
- 1/4 teaspoon ground ginger
- 1/4 teaspoon salt
- 1/2 teaspoon baking powder
- 1/2 teaspoon pure vanilla extract

DIRECTIONS:

1. Preheat your oven to 350°F (180°C) and line a baking sheet with parchment paper or a silicone baking mat.

2. In a large mixing bowl, combine the cooked quinoa, rolled oats, grated carrots, applesauce, honey (or maple syrup), raisins (or chopped dates), chopped walnuts, cinnamon, nutmeg, ginger, salt, baking powder, and vanilla extract. Stir until all the ingredients are well combined.

3. Drop rounded tablespoons of the dough onto the prepared baking sheet using a spoon or an ice cream scoop. Flatten each cookie slightly with the back of the spoon.

4. Bake the cookies for 22-25 minutes until the edges are golden brown and the cookies are firm to the touch.

5. Remove the cookies from the oven and allow them to cool on the baking sheet for 5 minutes before transferring them to a wire rack to cool completely.

Nutritional values: Calories: 130 kcal, Protein: 3 g, Carbohydrates: 22 g, Fiber: 2 g, Fat: 4 g, Saturated Fat: 0.5 g, Sodium: 85 mg, Potassium: 150 mg, Sugar: 9 g

ICE CREAM SUNDAE

 PREP TIME: 10 MINUTES   **SERVINGS: 4**

INGREDIENTS:

- 4 cups vanilla ice cream (or your favorite flavor)
- 1 cup hot fudge sauce, warmed
- 1 cup whipped cream
- 1/2 cup chopped nuts (such as almonds, pecans, or walnuts)
- 1/2 cup maraschino cherries
- **Optional toppings:** caramel sauce, sprinkles, crushed cookies, fresh fruit

DIRECTIONS:

1. Scoop 1 cup of ice cream into the four serving bowls or sundae dishes.
2. Drizzle each serving with 1/4 cup of warmed hot fudge sauce.
3. Top each sundae with 1/4 cup of whipped cream.
4. Sprinkle each sundae with 2 tablespoons of chopped nuts.
5. Add 2 maraschino cherries to each sundae for garnish.
6. If desired, add any additional toppings of your choice and serve immediately.

Nutritional values (without toppings): Calories: 620, Fat: 35g, Saturated Fat: 15g, Carbohydrates: 70g, Fiber: 3g, Protein: 10g, Cholesterol: 60mg, Sodium: 250mg, Sugar: 58g

NO-BAKE OATMEAL COOKIES

 PREP TIME: 5 MINUTES    **SERVINGS: 12 COOKIES**    **CHILLING TIME: 30 MINUTES**

INGREDIENTS:

- 1/2 cup unsalted butter
- 1/2 cup granulated sugar
- 1/2 cup packed light brown sugar
- 1/4 cup unsweetened cocoa powder
- 1/4 cup milk
- 1/4 cup smooth peanut butter
- 1 teaspoon pure vanilla extract
- 1 1/2 cups quick-cooking oats

DIRECTIONS:

1. Combine the butter, granulated sugar, brown sugar, cocoa powder, and milk in a medium saucepan over low heat. Stir until the butter is melted and the ingredients are well mixed.

2. Turn the heat up to medium and bring the mixture to a rolling boil. Cook for 1 minute, and then remove the saucepan from the heat.

3. Stir in the peanut butter and vanilla extract until smooth.

4. Fold in the quick-cooking oats, ensuring all the oats are coated with the mixture.

5. Line a baking sheet with parchment paper or wax paper.

6. Drop spoonfuls of the cookie mixture onto the lined baking sheet, creating approximately 12 cookies.

7. Allow the cookies to cool and harden at room temperature for about 30 minutes, or place them in the refrigerator to speed up the process.

Nutritional values: Calories: 220, Fat: 11g, Saturated Fat: 5g, Carbohydrates: 28g, Fiber: 2g, Protein: 4g, Cholesterol: 20mg, Sodium: 25mg, Sugar: 18g

CHOCOLATE PUDDING

 PREP TIME: 10 MINUTES   **SERVINGS: 4**    **COOK TIME: 10 MINUTES**
CHILL TIME: 2 HOURS

INGREDIENTS:

- 1/2 cup granulated sugar
- 1/4 cup unsweetened cocoa powder
- 1/4 cup cornstarch
- 1/4 teaspoon salt
- 2 cups whole milk
- 1 cup heavy cream
- 6 ounces semisweet chocolate, chopped
- 1 teaspoon pure vanilla extract

DIRECTIONS:

1. Whisk together the sugar, cocoa powder, cornstarch, and salt in a medium saucepan.

2. Gradually whisk in the milk and heavy cream until smooth and well combined.

3. Place the saucepan over medium heat and cook, constantly whisking, until the mixture thickens and comes to a gentle boil. This should take about 5-7 minutes.

4. Reduce the heat to low and cook for 2-3 minutes, constantly whisking to avoid lumps.

5. Remove the saucepan from the heat and add the chopped semisweet chocolate. Stir until the chocolate is completely melted and the mixture is smooth.

6. Stir in the vanilla extract.

7. Pour the pudding into four individual serving dishes or one large serving dish. Cover the surface of the pudding with plastic wrap to prevent skin from forming.

8. Refrigerate for at least 2 hours or until the pudding is chilled and set.

9. Serve chilled with whipped cream or fresh fruit as desired.

Nutritional values: Calories: 595, Fat: 38g, Saturated Fat: 22g, Carbohydrates: 62g, Fiber: 5g, Protein: 8g, Cholesterol: 80mg, Sodium: 210mg, Sugar: 47g

PEANUT BUTTER FUDGE

 PREP TIME: 10 MINUTES   **SERVINGS: 36 SQUARES**   **COOK TIME: 5 MINUTES**
CHILL TIME: 2 HOURS

INGREDIENTS:

- 1 cup unsalted butter
- 1 cup creamy peanut butter
- 1 teaspoon pure vanilla extract
- 1/4 teaspoon salt
- 4 cups powdered sugar, sifted

DIRECTIONS:

1. Line an 8x8-inch square baking pan with parchment paper, leaving an overhang on two sides for easy removal.

2. In a medium saucepan, combine the unsalted butter and peanut butter. Cook over low heat, stirring occasionally, until the butter and peanut butter are completely melted and well combined.

3. Remove the saucepan from the heat and stir in the vanilla extract and salt.

4. Gradually add the sifted powdered sugar to the peanut butter mixture, stirring until smooth and fully incorporated.

5. Pour the fudge mixture into the prepared baking pan and smooth the top with a spatula.

6. Refrigerate the fudge for at least 2 hours, or until it is firm and set.

7. Use the parchment paper overhang to lift the fudge out of the pan and transfer it to a cutting board. Cut the fudge into 36 equal squares.

8. Store the peanut butter fudge in an airtight container in the refrigerator for up to 2 weeks.

Nutritional values: Calories: 150, Fat: 9g, Saturated Fat: 4g, Carbohydrates: 17g, Protein: 2g, Cholesterol: 14mg, Sodium: 70mg, Sugar: 16g

BANANA BREAD

 PREP TIME: 15 MINUTES   **SERVINGS: 12 SLICES**   **COOK TIME: 60 MINUTES**

INGREDIENTS:

- 1 cup granulated sugar
- 1/2 cup unsalted butter, softened
- 2 large eggs
- 3 ripe bananas, mashed (about 1 1/2 cups)
- 1/4 cup milk
- 1 teaspoon pure vanilla extract
- 2 cups all-purpose flour
- 1 teaspoon baking powder
- 1/2 teaspoon baking soda
- 1/4 teaspoon salt
- 1/2 cup chopped walnuts or pecans (optional)

DIRECTIONS:

1. Preheat your oven to 350°F (175°C) and grease a 9x5-inch loaf pan.
2. In a large mixing bowl, cream together the granulated sugar and softened butter until light and fluffy.
3. Add the eggs, one at a time, mixing well after each addition.
4. Stir in the mashed bananas, milk, and vanilla extract until well combined.
5. Whisk together the all-purpose flour, baking powder, baking soda, and salt in a separate bowl.
6. Gradually add the dry and wet ingredients, mixing until just combined. Be careful not to overmix.
7. Fold in the chopped walnuts or pecans, if using.
8. Pour the batter into the prepared loaf pan and smooth the top with a spatula.
9. Bake for 60-65 minutes, or until a toothpick inserted into the center of the bread comes out clean.
10. Remove the banana bread from the oven and let it cool in the pan for 10 minutes before transferring it to a wire rack to cool completely.

Nutritional values: Calories: 260, Fat: 10g, Saturated Fat: 6g, Carbohydrates: 40g, Fiber: 1g, Protein: 4g, Cholesterol: 53mg, Sodium: 180mg, Sugar: 22g

ALMOND FLOUR CHOCOLATE CHIP COOKIES

 PREP TIME: 15 MINUTES    **SERVINGS: 24 COOKIES**    **COOK TIME: 12-14 MINUTES**

INGREDIENTS:

- 2 cups almond flour
- 1/2 teaspoon baking soda
- 1/4 teaspoon salt
- 1/3 cup coconut oil, melted
- 1/4 cup maple syrup
- 1 teaspoon vanilla extract
- 1 large egg
- 1 cup semisweet chocolate chips

DIRECTIONS:

1. Preheat your oven to 350°F (180°C) and line two baking sheets with parchment paper or silicone mats.

2. Whisk together the almond flour, baking soda, and salt in a medium-sized bowl.

3. Combine the melted coconut oil, maple syrup, vanilla extract, and egg in a separate bowl. Mix well.

4. Add the wet ingredients to the dry ingredients and stir until fully combined. Fold in the chocolate chips.

5. Scoop about a tablespoon of dough for each cookie and place it on the prepared baking sheets, spacing them about 2 inches apart. Flatten the cookies slightly with your fingers or the back of a spoon.

6. Bake for 12-14 minutes or until the edges are golden brown. Be cautious not to over-bake, as almond flour can burn easily.

7. Remove from the oven and let the cookies cool on the baking sheets for about 5 minutes before transferring them to a wire rack to cool completely.

Nutritional values: Calories: 135, Fat: 10g, Saturated Fat: 4g, Carbohydrates: 10g, Fiber: 1g, Sugar: 7g, Protein: 3g

SMART DRINKING: SMOOTHIES AND JUICES

Let me tell you, I've been there: late-night study sessions, endless classes, and balancing a social life. It's all too easy to fall into the trap of grabbing that extra cup of coffee or chomping down on fast food just to keep us going. But what if I told you there's a better way to get through those hectic days? That's right—smoothies and juices are here to save the day, and your college experience!

Now, I know what you're thinking: "Smoothies? Juices? Who has time for that?" Well, the truth is, it's not as time-consuming as you think. In fact, it's a pretty cool way to get in all those fruits, veggies, and nutrients we so desperately need while living that campus life. Plus, it's much more budget-friendly than buying pre-made smoothies or going to the juice bar on a daily basis.

I remember when I first discovered the magical power of smoothies. During my sophomore year, I had just pulled an all-nighter studying for a chemistry exam. I was exhausted, anxious, and in desperate need of energy to get through the day. Instead of my customary bagel and cream cheese, I gave the smoothie craze a try. I blended spinach, a banana, and almond milk until smooth, and voilà! I was immediately hooked.

Not only did it taste amazing, but I also noticed a significant difference in my energy levels and overall mood. As the days passed, I started experimenting with different fruits, veggies, and other ingredients. I even got my roommates in on the action, and we had a great time making tasty and nutritious smoothies and juices together. We transformed our kitchen into a small smoothie lab, swapping recipes, rating one other's creations, and challenging each other to try new ingredients. It became a small college ritual for us.

Smoothies and juices, however, are about more than just having fun and socializing with your roommates and buddies—they're also about caring for your health and mind. Maintaining a healthy diet and staying hydrated is essential when juggling coursework, extracurriculars, and social lives. Smoothies and juices are wonderful ways to accomplish this. They give a simple, practical, and enjoyable way to take essential nutrients, vitamins, and minerals our bodies require to function at their best.

We all know that the "broke college student" stereotype exists for a reason: every penny counts. Making your own drinks at home can save you some serious dough. Investing in a blender and some basic ingredients will save you money down the road while also helping the environment by reducing waste from store-bought drinks.

So, are you ready to dive into the world of smoothies and juices?

BASICS

Let's get down to the nitty-gritty of smoothie and juice making. Don't worry; it's not rocket science! With the right equipment, ingredients, and some know-how, you'll be a smoothie and juice whiz in no time. So, let's get started and get you on your way to becoming the perfect smoothie and juice connoisseur!

First things first: equipment. You don't need a fancy, high-end blender or juicer to make great smoothies and juices, but you do need something reliable and efficient. There are plenty of budget-friendly options out there that work just fine. A basic blender with a few smoothie speed options should suffice. There are manual and electric juicers available, so pick what fits your budget and preferences. Let's take a moment to consider the environment. We'd all like to do our share to reduce waste, right? Consider purchasing reusable straws and storage containers. These will help reduce single-use plastics while also making it very simple to take your delectable creations on the go!

Next up: ingredients. The possibilities for smoothies and juices are endless, but choosing the right ingredients is essential to ensure you're getting the most Nutritional bang for your buck. Fresh vs. frozen? Organic vs. non-organic? Here's the scoop: Fresh produce is excellent, but sometimes, it's not practical. Frozen fruits and veggies are a fantastic alternative because they're picked at peak ripeness and quickly frozen, locking in their nutrients. Also, they are frequently more affordable and have a better shelf life.

The decision between organic and non-organic food is ultimately yours. Organic fruit contains less pesticides but is more expensive. If money is an issue, try buying organic for the "Dirty Dozen" (the fruits and vegetables with the highest pesticide residue) and conventional for the "Clean Fifteen" (those with the lowest residue).

Now, let's discuss liquid bases. Your choice of the base can make a huge difference in the taste and texture of your smoothie or juice. Milk, yogurt, water, and juice are all good popular options. Each base has its benefits: milk and yogurt add creaminess and a dose of calcium and protein, while the water keeps things lighter and low-calorie. Juice can provide a rush of flavor and extra vitamins, but try to minimize added sugars and stick to 100% fruit juice.

Speaking of sugar, let's address sweeteners. While it may be tempting to fill up your smoothie or drink with sugar to satisfy your sweet tooth, healthier choices will not have the same effect on your waistline. You can use natural sweeteners like honey, maple syrup, or dates. Even better, let your fruits' natural sweetness do the job!

And there you have it—the fundamentals of smoothies and juices! With this knowledge, you may begin your healthy and tasty trip. Remember that the key is to experiment and learn what works best for you. Now, my friends, go forth and blend!

ENERGIZING BREAKFAST SMOOTHIES

MORNING POWERHOUSE

 PREP TIME: 5 MINUTES **SERVINGS: 2**

INGREDIENTS:

- 1 cup fresh spinach, packed
- 1 medium ripe banana, peeled
- 1 cup frozen mixed berries
- 1 tablespoon chia seeds
- 1 tablespoon almond butter
- 1 cup unsweetened almond milk
- 1/4 cup rolled oats
- 1 teaspoon honey (optional)

DIRECTIONS:

1. In a blender, add the spinach, banana, frozen mixed berries, chia seeds, almond butter, unsweetened almond milk, and rolled oats.

2. Blend on high speed until smooth and creamy. If the smoothie is too thick, add more almond milk until you reach your desired consistency. If you prefer a sweeter smoothie, add honey to taste.

3. Pour the smoothie into two glasses, and serve immediately. Enjoy your smoothie!

Nutritional values: Calories: 260, Total Fat: 10g, Sodium: 125mg, Dietary Fiber: 9g, Sugars: 20g, Protein: 8g, Calcium: 320mg, Iron: 2mg, Potassium: 550mg

SUNRISE CITRUS SURPRISE

 PREP TIME: 5 MINUTES **SERVINGS: 2**

INGREDIENTS:

- 1 large orange, peeled and segmented
- 1 medium grapefruit, peeled and segmented
- 1 small lemon, peeled and seeded
- 1 small lime, peeled and seeded
- 1 medium carrot, peeled and chopped
- 1 cup frozen pineapple chunks
- 1 cup unsweetened almond milk (or any milk of choice)
- 1 tbsp honey or agave syrup (optional)
- A handful of ice cubes (optional)

DIRECTIONS:

1. In a blender, combine the orange, grapefruit, lemon, lime, carrot, pineapple, almond milk, and honey or agave syrup (if using).

2. Blend on high speed until smooth and creamy. Add ice cubes to reach your desired consistency and blend again if needed.

3. Taste the smoothie and adjust the sweetness if necessary.

4. Pour the smoothie into two glasses and serve immediately.

Nutritional values: Calories: 210, Total Fat: 2g , Cholesterol: 0mg, Sodium: 130mg, Dietary Fiber: 6g, Total Sugars: 34g, Protein: 4g, Vitamin D: 2mcg, Calcium: 350mg, Iron: 0.8mg, Potassium: 650mg

ALMOND OAT BLISS

 PREP TIME: 5 MINUTES   **SERVINGS: 2**

INGREDIENTS:

- 1 cup unsweetened almond milk
- 1/2 cup rolled oats (old-fashioned or quick oats)
- 1 medium ripe banana, frozen or fresh
- 1/4 cup plain Greek yogurt
- 2 tbsp almond butter
- 1 tbsp honey or maple syrup (optional)
- 1/2 tsp vanilla extract
- 1/4 tsp ground cinnamon

DIRECTIONS:

1. In a blender, combine the almond milk and rolled oats. Blend for about 30 seconds or until the oats are broken down and have a smooth texture.
2. Add the banana, Greek yogurt, almond butter, honey or maple syrup (if using), vanilla extract, and ground cinnamon to the blender. Blend until smooth and creamy.
3. Pour the smoothie into two glasses, garnish with a sprinkle of cinnamon or a few almond slices, and enjoy!

Nutritional values: Calories: 330 kcal, Protein: 12 g, Fat: 16 g, Dietary Fiber: 6 g, Sugars: 15 g, Cholesterol: 3 mg, Sodium: 110 mg, Potassium: 480 mg

JAVA JOLT SMOOTHIE

 PREP TIME: 5 MINUTES   **SERVINGS: 2**

INGREDIENTS:

- 1 cup brewed coffee, chilled
- 1 ripe banana, sliced
- 1/2 cup unsweetened almond milk (or milk of your choice)
- 1 scoop (about 30g) of chocolate or vanilla protein powder
- 1 tablespoon unsweetened cocoa powder
- 1 tablespoon almond butter (or nut butter of your choice)
- 1 cup ice cubes
- Optional: 1 teaspoon of honey or maple syrup for added sweetness

DIRECTIONS:

1. In a blender, combine the chilled coffee, sliced banana, almond milk, protein powder, cocoa powder, almond butter, and ice cubes.
2. Blend on high speed until smooth and creamy. If the smoothie is too thick, add more almond milk or a little water to achieve the desired consistency.
3. Taste the smoothie and add honey or maple syrup if desired for added sweetness. Blend again for a few seconds to mix in the sweetener.
4. Pour the smoothie into two glasses, and serve immediately. Enjoy your energizing smoothie!

Nutritional values: Calories: 250, Protein: 20g, Fiber: 5g, Sugars: 15g, Fat: 10g, Sodium: 180mg, Potassium: 500mg

IMMUNITY BOOSTING JUICES

VITAMIN C BOOSTER

 PREP TIME: 10 MINUTES   **SERVINGS: 2**

INGREDIENTS:

- 1 large orange, peeled and segmented
- 2 medium-sized kiwis, peeled and sliced
- 1 cup fresh or frozen strawberries, hulled
- 1/2 cup pineapple chunks, fresh or frozen
- 1 small lemon, peeled and seeded
- 1/2-inch piece of fresh ginger peeled
- 1 cup cold water (optional, for a thinner juice consistency)

DIRECTIONS:

1. Prepare your fruits by washing, peeling, and cutting them as needed.
2. If you're using a juicer, run the orange, kiwi, strawberries, pineapple, lemon, and ginger through the juicer according to the manufacturer's instructions. Stir the juice to combine the flavors and, if desired, add water to thin the consistency.
3. If you're using a blender, add the prepared fruits and ginger to the blender, along with the cold water. Blend on high speed until smooth. Use a fine mesh strainer or nut milk bag to strain the juice, discarding the pulp and seeds.
4. Pour the Vitamin C Booster juice into two glasses and serve immediately.

Nutritional values: Calories: 150, Protein: 2g, Fiber: 6g, Sugars: 27g, Fat: 1g , Sodium: 5mg, Potassium: 670mg, Vitamin C: 280% Daily Value

ANTIOXIDANT ELIXIR

 PREP TIME: 10 MINUTES   **SERVINGS: 2**

INGREDIENTS:

- 1 cup fresh blueberries
- 1 cup fresh strawberries, hulled and halved
- 1 cup fresh spinach leaves, packed
- 1 medium beet, peeled and chopped
- 1/2 medium lemon, peeled and deseeded
- 1-inch piece of fresh ginger, peeled
- 1 cup water or coconut water
- Optional: 1 teaspoon of honey or maple syrup for added sweetness

DIRECTIONS:

1. Rinse and prepare the blueberries, strawberries, spinach, beet, lemon, and ginger as instructed.
2. Using a juicer, juice the blueberries, strawberries, spinach, beet, lemon, and ginger according to the manufacturer's instructions. If you don't have a juicer, use a high-speed blender and strain the juice using a fine-mesh sieve or nut milk bag.
3. Pour the juice into a large glass or pitcher, and add water or coconut water to dilute the juice to your desired consistency.
4. Taste the juice and add honey or maple syrup if desired for added sweetness. Stir well to combine.
5. Pour the Antioxidant Elixir into two glasses and serve immediately.

Nutritional values: Calories: 100, Protein: 2g, Fiber: 5g , Sugars: 15g, Fat: 0.5g, Sodium: 60mg, Potassium: 480mg

GREEN DEFENDER

 PREP TIME: 10 MINUTES   **SERVINGS: 2**

INGREDIENTS:

- 2 cups fresh spinach
- 2 cups kale leaves, stems removed
- 1 medium cucumber, chopped
- 2 medium green apples, cored and chopped
- 1 lemon, peeled
- 1-inch piece of fresh ginger, peeled
- Optional: 1 tablespoon of honey or maple syrup for added sweetness

DIRECTIONS:

1. Wash and prepare all produce, ensuring it's free from dirt and debris.
2. Feed the spinach, kale, cucumber, green apples, lemon, and ginger through the juicer, catching the juice in a container.
3. If desired, add honey or maple syrup to the juice for added sweetness, and stir well to combine.
4. Pour the juice into two glasses, and serve immediately for the best taste and maximum nutrient content.

Nutritional values: Calories: 120, Protein: 3g, Fiber: 1g, Sugars: 22g, Fat: 0.5g, Sodium: 60mg, Potassium: 520mg, Vitamin A: 120% DV, Vitamin C: 200% DV

SPICY GINGER ZING

 PREP TIME: 10 MINUTES   **SERVINGS: 2**

INGREDIENTS:

- 4 large carrots, peeled and chopped
- 2 oranges, peeled and seeded
- 1 medium apple, cored and chopped
- 1 lemon, peeled
- 1-inch piece of fresh ginger, peeled
- 1/4 teaspoon ground turmeric
- A pinch of black pepper
- **Optional:** 1 tablespoon of honey or maple syrup for added sweetness

DIRECTIONS:

1. Prepare your juicer according to the manufacturer's instructions.
2. Wash and prepare all produce, ensuring it's free from dirt and debris.
3. Feed the carrots, oranges, apple, lemon, and ginger through the juicer, catching the juice in a container.
4. Stir in the ground turmeric and a pinch of black pepper to the juice.
5. If desired, add honey or maple syrup to the juice for added sweetness, and stir well to combine.
6. Pour the juice into two glasses, and serve immediately for the best taste and maximum nutrient content.

Nutritional values: Calories: 180, Protein: 3g, Fiber: 7g, Sugars: 34g, Fat: 0.5g, Sodium: 100mg, Potassium: 800mg, Vitamin A: 410% DV, Vitamin C: 150% DV

POST-WORKOUT RECOVERY SMOOTHIES

MUSCLE MEND MAGIC

 PREP TIME: 5 MINUTES   **SERVINGS: 2**

INGREDIENTS:

- 1 cup frozen mixed berries (strawberries, blueberries, raspberries, and/or blackberries)
- 1 medium banana, sliced
- 1 cup plain Greek yogurt
- 1/2 cup unsweetened almond milk (or milk of your choice)
- 1 scoop (about 30g) vanilla or unflavored protein powder
- 2 tablespoons ground flaxseed
- 1 tablespoon chia seeds
- Optional: 1 teaspoon of honey or maple syrup for added sweetness

DIRECTIONS:

1. In a blender, combine the frozen mixed berries, sliced banana, Greek yogurt, almond milk, protein powder, ground flaxseed, and chia seeds.
2. Blend on high speed until smooth and creamy. If the smoothie is too thick, add more almond milk or a little water to achieve the desired consistency.
3. Taste the smoothie and add honey or maple syrup if desired for added sweetness. Blend again for a few seconds to mix in the sweetener.
4. Pour the smoothie into two glasses, and serve immediately.

Nutritional values: Calories: 330, Protein: 28g, Carbohydrates: 42g, Fiber: 9g, Sugars: 24g, Fat: 8g, Sodium: 180mg, Potassium: 600mg

REPLENISHING ELECTROLYTE FUSION

 PREP TIME: 5 MINUTES   **SERVINGS: 2**

INGREDIENTS:

- 1 medium banana, sliced
- 1 cup fresh or frozen mango chunks
- 1 cup coconut water (preferably with no added sugar)
- 1 cup unsweetened almond milk (or milk of your choice)
- 1 tablespoon chia seeds
- 1/2 of a medium avocado, peeled and pitted
- 1 cup ice cubes

DIRECTIONS:

1. In a blender, combine the banana, mango, coconut water, almond milk, chia seeds, avocado, and ice cubes.
2. Blend on high speed until smooth and creamy. If the smoothie is too thick, add more coconut water or almond milk to achieve the desired consistency.
3. Pour the smoothie into two glasses, and serve immediately. Enjoy your replenishing smoothie!

Nutritional values: Calories: 220, Protein: 4g, Fiber: 9g, Sugars: 20g, Fat: 9g, Sodium: 180mg, Potassium: 700mg

STRAWBERRY-BANANA REVIVE

 PREP TIME: 5 MINUTES  SERVINGS: 2

INGREDIENTS:

- 1 cup fresh or frozen strawberries
- 1 ripe banana, sliced
- 1 cup Greek yogurt (or yogurt of your choice)
- 1/2 cup unsweetened almond milk (or milk of your choice)
- 1 scoop (about 30g) of vanilla protein powder
- 1 tablespoon chia seeds
- **Optional:** 1 teaspoon of honey or maple syrup for added sweetness

DIRECTIONS:

1. In a blender, combine the strawberries, sliced banana, Greek yogurt, almond milk, protein powder, and chia seeds.
2. Blend on high speed until smooth and creamy. If the smoothie is too thick, add more almond milk or a little water to achieve the desired consistency.
3. Taste the smoothie and add honey or maple syrup if desired for added sweetness. Blend again for a few seconds to mix in the sweetener.
4. Pour the smoothie into two glasses, and serve immediately.

Nutritional values: Calories: 280, Protein: 26g, Fiber: 6g Sugars: 22g, Fat: 6g , Sodium: 180mg, Potassium: 600mg

COOL CUCUMBER RECOVERY

 PREP TIME: 5 MINUTES SERVINGS: 2

INGREDIENTS:

- 1 medium cucumber, peeled and chopped
- 1 cup fresh or frozen pineapple chunks
- 1 ripe avocado, pitted and peeled
- 1 cup baby spinach
- 1 scoop (about 30g) of vanilla protein powder
- 1 cup coconut water
- 1 cup ice cubes (skip if using frozen pineapple)

DIRECTIONS:

1. In a blender, combine the chopped cucumber, pineapple chunks, avocado, spinach, protein powder, coconut water, and ice cubes (if using).
2. Blend on high speed until smooth and creamy. If the smoothie is too thick, add more coconut water or a little water to achieve the desired consistency.
3. Pour the smoothie into two glasses, serve immediately, and enjoy!

Nutritional values: Calories: 300, Protein: 20g, Fiber: 10g, Sugars: 18g, Fat: 12g, Sodium: 180mg, Potassium: 980mg

QUICK AND HEALTHY SNACK SMOOTHIES

BERRYLICIOUS BLAST

 PREP TIME: 5 MINUTES  SERVINGS: 2

INGREDIENTS:

- 1 cup frozen mixed berries (such as blueberries, raspberries, and blackberries)
- 1 medium ripe banana, peeled and sliced
- 1 cup baby spinach, washed
- 1/2 cup Greek yogurt, plain or vanilla
- 1 cup unsweetened almond milk or milk of choice
- 1 tablespoon honey or maple syrup (optional)
- 1 tablespoon chia seeds (optional)

DIRECTIONS:

1. In a blender, combine the frozen mixed berries, sliced banana, baby spinach, Greek yogurt, almond milk, honey or maple syrup (if using), and chia seeds (if using).
2. Blend on high speed until smooth and creamy, stopping to scrape down the sides of the blender as needed. If the smoothie is too thick, add more almond milk to reach the desired consistency.
3. Pour the smoothie into two glasses and serve immediately.

Nutritional values: Calories: 202 kcal, Total Fat: 4 g, Sodium: 129 mg, Potassium: 528 mg, Total Carbohydrate: 36 g, Dietary Fiber: 6 g, Sugars: 24 g (less if not using sweetener), Protein: 9 g

TROPICAL ISLAND BREEZE

 PREP TIME: 5 MINUTES SERVINGS: 2

INGREDIENTS:

- 1 cup frozen pineapple chunks
- 1 cup frozen mango chunks
- 1 medium ripe banana, peeled and sliced
- 1 cup unsweetened coconut milk (or milk of choice)
- 1/2 cup orange juice
- 1 tablespoon honey or agave syrup (optional)
- 1 tablespoon flax seeds (optional)
- 1/4 cup unsweetened shredded coconut (optional for garnish)

DIRECTIONS:

1. In a blender, combine the frozen pineapple chunks, frozen mango chunks, sliced banana, coconut milk, orange juice, honey or agave syrup (if using), and flax seeds (if using).
2. Blend on high speed until smooth and creamy, stopping to scrape down the sides of the blender as needed. If the smoothie is too thick, add more coconut milk or orange juice to reach the desired consistency.
3. Pour the smoothie into two glasses. If desired, garnish with a sprinkle of unsweetened shredded coconut, and serve.

Nutritional values: Calories: 305 kcal, Total Fat: 12 g, Sodium: 41 mg, Potassium: 680 mg, Total Carbohydrate: 49 g, Dietary, Fiber: 5 g, Sugars: 37 g (less if not using sweetener), Protein: 3 g

SPINACH-APPLE REFRESHER

 PREP TIME: 5 MINUTES    SERVINGS: 2

INGREDIENTS:

- 2 cups baby spinach, washed
- 1 medium green apple, cored and chopped
- 1 medium ripe banana, peeled and sliced
- 1/2 cup cucumber, peeled and chopped
- 1 cup unsweetened almond milk (or milk of choice)
- 1/2 cup ice cubes
- 1 tablespoon honey or agave syrup (optional)
- 1 tablespoon chia seeds (optional)
- Fresh mint leaves (optional, for garnish)

DIRECTIONS:

1. In a blender, combine the baby spinach, chopped green apple, sliced banana, chopped cucumber, almond milk, ice cubes, honey or agave syrup (if using), and chia seeds (if using).

2. Blend on high speed until smooth and creamy, stopping to scrape down the sides of the blender as needed. If the smoothie is too thick, add more almond milk to reach the desired consistency.

3. Pour the smoothie into two glasses. Garnish with a few fresh mint leaves, and serve immediately if desired.

Nutritional values: Calories: 175 kcal, Total Fat: 3 g, Sodium: 123 mg, Potassium: 594 mg, Total Carbohydrate: 37 g, Dietary Fiber: 7 g, Sugars: 24 g (less if not using sweetener), Protein: 4 g

NUTTY NECTAR DELIGHT

 PREP TIME: 5 MINUTES   SERVINGS: 2

DIRECTIONS:

INGREDIENTS:

- 1 cup frozen peach slices
- 1/2 cup frozen mixed berries (such as blueberries, raspberries, and blackberries)
- 1 medium ripe banana, peeled and sliced
- 1/4 cup almond butter (or nut butter of choice)
- 1 cup unsweetened almond milk (or milk of choice)
- 1/2 cup pure apple juice (or additional almond milk)
- 1 tablespoon honey or maple syrup (optional)
- 1 tablespoon ground flaxseed (optional)
- 2 tablespoons chopped nuts (such as almonds, walnuts, or pecans, optional, for garnish)

1. In a blender, combine the frozen peach slices, frozen mixed berries, sliced banana, almond butter, almond milk, apple juice, honey, or maple syrup (if using), and ground flaxseed (if using).

2. Blend on high speed until smooth and creamy, stopping to scrape down the sides of the blender as needed. If the smoothie is too thick, add more almond milk or apple juice to reach the desired consistency.

3. Pour the smoothie into two glasses. Garnish with a sprinkle of chopped nuts if desired, and serve immediately.

Nutritional values: Calories: 342 kcal, Total Fat: 18 g, Sodium: 96 mg, Potassium: 637 mg, Total Carbohydrate: 43 g, Dietary Fiber: 8 g, Sugars: 29 g (less if not using sweetener), Protein: 9 g

DESSERT-INSPIRED SMOOTHIES AND JUICES

VELVETY CHOCOLATE INDULGENCE

 PREP TIME: 5 MINUTES   **SERVINGS: 2**

INGREDIENTS:

- 1 medium ripe banana, peeled and sliced
- 1 cup unsweetened vanilla almond milk (or milk of choice)
- 1/2 cup Greek yogurt (plain or vanilla-flavored)
- 1/4 cup unsweetened cocoa powder
- 2 tablespoons honey or maple syrup (adjust to taste)
- 1/2 teaspoon pure vanilla extract
- 1 cup ice cubes
- Whipped cream or whipped coconut cream (optional, for garnish)
- Chocolate shavings (optional, for garnish)

DIRECTIONS:

1. Combine the sliced banana, almond milk, Greek yogurt, unsweetened cocoa powder, honey or maple syrup, vanilla extract, and ice cubes in a blender.
2. Blend on high speed until smooth and creamy, stopping to scrape down the sides of the blender as needed. If the smoothie is too thick, add more almond milk to reach the desired consistency.
3. Taste the smoothie and adjust the sweetness by adding more honey or maple syrup if needed.
4. Pour the smoothie into two glasses. Garnish with a dollop of whipped cream or coconut cream and a sprinkle of chocolate shavings if desired.
5. Serve immediately.

Nutritional values: Calories: 220 kcal, Total Fat: 4.5 g, Saturated Fat: 1 g, Sodium: 102 mg, Potassium: 495 mg, Total Carbohydrate: 42 g, Dietary Fiber: 5 g, Sugars: 29 g (less if using less sweetener), Protein: 9 g

RASPBERRY CHEESECAKE DREAM

 PREP TIME: 5 MINUTES    **SERVINGS: 2**

INGREDIENTS:

- 1 cup fresh or frozen raspberries
- 1/2 cup Greek yogurt (plain or vanilla-flavored)
- 1/4 cup cream cheese, softened
- 1 cup unsweetened almond milk (or milk of choice)
- 2 tablespoons honey or maple syrup (adjust to taste)
- 1/2 teaspoon pure vanilla extract
- 1 cup ice cubes
- Fresh raspberries and graham cracker crumbs (optional, for garnish)

DIRECTIONS:

1. Combine the raspberries, Greek yogurt, softened cream cheese, almond milk, honey or maple syrup, vanilla extract, and ice cubes in a blender.

2. Blend on high speed until smooth and creamy, stopping to scrape down the sides of the blender as needed. If the smoothie is too thick, add more almond milk to reach the desired consistency.

3. Taste the smoothie and adjust the sweetness by adding more honey or maple syrup if needed.

4. Pour the smoothie into two glasses. If desired, garnish with a few fresh raspberries and a sprinkle of graham cracker crumbs. Serve immediately.

Nutritional values: Calories: 295 kcal, Total Fat: 13 g, Saturated Fat: 7 g, Sodium: 195 mg, Potassium: 290 mg, Total Carbohydrate: 37 g, Dietary Fiber: 4 g, Sugars: 30 g (less if using less sweetener), Protein: 9 g

CINNAMON ROLL SENSATION

 PREP TIME: 10 MINUTES   **SERVINGS: 2 SMOOTHIES**

INGREDIENTS:

- 1 cup unsweetened almond milk
- 1 large ripe banana, frozen
- 1/4 cup rolled oats
- 2 tablespoons almond butter
- 1 tablespoon honey or maple syrup (adjust to taste)
- 1 teaspoon ground cinnamon
- 1/4 teaspoon ground nutmeg
- 1/2 teaspoon pure vanilla extract
- 1 cup ice cubes
- **Optional:** whipped cream and a pinch of cinnamon for garnish

DIRECTIONS:

1. Combine the almond milk, frozen banana, rolled oats, almond butter, honey or maple syrup, ground cinnamon, ground nutmeg, and vanilla extract in a blender.

2. Blend the mixture on high speed until smooth and creamy. If the consistency is too thick, add a little more almond milk and blend again.

3. Add the ice cubes to the blender and blend again until the smoothie reaches your desired consistency.

4. Pour the Cinnamon Roll Sensation Smoothie into two glasses. Top with whipped cream and a sprinkle of cinnamon for garnish if desired. Serve immediately and enjoy!

Nutritional values: Calories: 280 kcal, Fat: 13 g, Carbohydrates: 37 g, Protein: 7 g, Sodium: 95 mg, Fiber: 6 g, Sugar: 19 g

PINA COLADA PARADISE

 PREP TIME: 10 MINUTES   **SERVINGS: 2 SMOOTHIES**

INGREDIENTS:

- 1 1/2 cups frozen pineapple chunks
- 1/2 cup coconut milk (canned, full-fat recommended)
- 1/2 cup unsweetened almond milk or coconut water
- 1/2 cup Greek yogurt (vanilla or plain)
- 1 tablespoon honey or maple syrup (adjust to taste)
- 1/2 teaspoon pure vanilla extract
- 1/4 teaspoon coconut extract (optional)
- 1 cup ice cubes
- **Optional:** pineapple wedges and unsweetened shredded coconut for garnish

DIRECTIONS:

1. In a blender, combine the frozen pineapple chunks, coconut milk, almond milk or coconut water, Greek yogurt, honey or maple syrup, vanilla extract, and coconut extract (if using).

2. Blend the mixture on high speed until smooth and creamy. If the consistency is too thick, add a little more almond milk or coconut water and blend again.

3. Add the ice cubes to the blender and blend again until the smoothie reaches your desired consistency.

4. Pour the Pina Colada Paradise Smoothie into two glasses. Garnish with pineapple wedges and a sprinkle of unsweetened shredded coconut if desired.

5. Serve immediately and enjoy your tropical escape!

Nutritional values: Calories: 280 kcal, Fat: 12 g, Carbohydrates: 37 g, Protein: 8 g, Sodium: 60 mg, Fiber: 3 g, Sugar: 29 g

REFRESHING JUICES

SUMMER SPLASH

 PREP TIME: 10 MINUTES   **SERVINGS: 2 SMOOTHIES**

INGREDIENTS:

- 1 1/2 cups frozen pineapple chunks
- 1/2 cup coconut milk (canned, full-fat recommended)
- 1/2 cup unsweetened almond milk or coconut water
- 1/2 cup Greek yogurt (vanilla or plain)
- 1 tablespoon honey or maple syrup (adjust to taste)
- 1/2 teaspoon pure vanilla extract
- 1/4 teaspoon coconut extract (optional)
- 1 cup ice cubes
- **Optional:** pineapple wedges and unsweetened shredded coconut for garnish

DIRECTIONS:

1. In a blender, combine the frozen pineapple chunks, coconut milk, almond milk or coconut water, Greek yogurt, honey or maple syrup, vanilla extract, and coconut extract (if using).
2. Blend the mixture on high speed until smooth and creamy. If the consistency is too thick, add a little more almond milk or coconut water and blend again.
3. Add the ice cubes to the blender and blend again until the smoothie reaches your desired consistency.
4. Pour the Pina Colada Paradise Smoothie into two glasses. Garnish with pineapple wedges and a sprinkle of unsweetened shredded coconut if desired. Serve immediately and enjoy your tropical escape!

Nutritional values: Calories: 280 kcal, Fat: 12 g, Carbohydrates: 37 g, Protein: 8 g, Sodium: 60 mg, Fiber: 3 g, Sugar: 29 g

WATERMELON MINT COOLER

 PREP TIME: 10 MINUTES    **SERVINGS: 4**

INGREDIENTS:

- 4 cups fresh watermelon, cubed and seedless
- 1 cup fresh mint leaves, plus extra for garnish
- 1/4 cup fresh lime juice (approximately two limes)
- 1 cup sparkling water or club soda
- 1 cup crushed ice
- **Optional:** 2 tablespoons honey or agave syrup for additional sweetness (if needed)

DIRECTIONS:

1. Combine the watermelon, mint leaves, and lime juice in a blender. Blend until smooth and well combined.
2. Using a fine mesh strainer, strain the mixture into a large pitcher to remove any pulp or seeds.
3. Taste the mixture and add honey or agave syrup if additional sweetness is desired.
4. Add crushed ice and sparkling water or club soda to the pitcher. Stir gently to combine, maintaining the fizz from the sparkling water.
5. Pour the Watermelon Mint Cooler into four glasses, garnish with a sprig of mint, and serve immediately. Enjoy this refreshing and hydrating beverage on a hot summer day or at your next outdoor gathering.

Nutritional values: Calories: 80 kcal, Total Fat: 0.2g, Sodium: 25mg, Total Carbohydrate: 19g, Dietary Fiber: 1g, Total Sugars: 17g, Protein: 1g

PINEAPPLE GINGER ZEST

 PREP TIME: 10 MINUTES   **SERVINGS: 4**

INGREDIENTS:

- 4 cups fresh pineapple, cubed
- 2 cups cold water
- 1/4 cup fresh ginger, peeled and roughly chopped
- 2 tablespoons fresh lemon juice (approximately 1 lemon)
- 1 tablespoon honey or agave syrup (adjust to taste)
- 1 cup crushed ice
- **Optional:** pineapple wedges and lemon slices for garnish

DIRECTIONS:

1. Combine the pineapple, water, ginger, and lemon juice in a blender. Blend until smooth and well combined.

2. Using a fine mesh strainer, strain the mixture into a large pitcher to remove any pulp or fibrous ginger pieces.

3. Add the honey or agave syrup to the pitcher and stir until dissolved.

4. Add the crushed ice to the pitcher and stir to combine.

5. Pour the Pineapple Ginger Zest into four glasses, garnish with pineapple wedges and lemon slices if desired, and serve immediately. Enjoy this zesty and revitalizing beverage on a warm day or as a pick-me-up at any time.

Nutritional values: Calories: 120 kcal, Total Fat: 0.2g, Sodium: 10mg, Total Carbohydrate: 31g, Dietary Fiber: 2g, Total Sugars: 26g, Protein: 1g

CUCUMBER-LIME QUENCHER

 PREP TIME: 10 MINUTES    **SERVINGS: 4**

INGREDIENTS:

- 2 large cucumbers, peeled and roughly chopped
- 1/4 cup fresh lime juice (approximately 2 limes)
- 4 cups cold water
- 2 tablespoons honey or agave syrup (adjust to taste)
- 1 cup crushed ice
- **Optional:** cucumber slices and lime wedges for garnish

DIRECTIONS:

1. In a blender, combine the cucumbers, lime juice, and water. Blend until smooth and well combined.
2. Using a fine mesh strainer, strain the mixture into a large pitcher to remove any pulp or cucumber seeds.
3. Add the honey or agave syrup to the pitcher and stir until dissolved.
4. Add the crushed ice to the pitcher and stir to combine.
5. Pour the Cucumber-Lime Quencher into four glasses, garnish with cucumber slices and lime wedges if desired, and serve immediately.

Nutritional values: Calories: 70 kcal, Total Fat: 0.2g, Sodium: 10mg, Total Carbohydrate: 17g, Dietary Fiber: 1g, Total Sugars: 14g, Protein: 1g

SOCIAL COOKING: THE ART OF CULINARY CONNECTION

Get ready to dive into one of the most enjoyable and memorable aspects of college life: social cooking! This fun chapter will go through group-friendly dishes, hosting potlucks and themed dinners, and catering to everyone's dietary needs.

During my college years, some of my dearest and funniest memories were made in the kitchen, surrounded by friends. We'd gather in our tiny dorm kitchens or communal cooking spaces and whip up tasty, budget-friendly meals together. Those evenings spent laughing, telling stories, and bonding over food are memories I'll cherish for the rest of my life. Those experiences inspired me to write this chapter and share the joy of social cooking with you.

First, we'll look at Group-Friendly Meals that are ideal for cooking and sharing with your friends. These recipes are simple to make and ideal for entertaining a large group. Plus, they are designed to be customizable, allowing everyone to build their own gourmet masterpiece! I've got classics like pizza, tacos, and fajitas as well as more experimental options like DIY sushi rolls.

Then, we'll dive into hosting potlucks and themed dinners. This is where you may let your imagination run wild and gather folks around the dinner table. I still remember the legendary "Taco Tuesday" nights we used to have in our dorm - the aroma of sizzling spices and freshly chopped ingredients filled the corridors, luring everyone in to join the feast. This section will provide planning tips, recipe suggestions, and advice on accommodating allergen and dietary requirements so that everyone has a lovely time.

One of the best things about social cooking is that it fills not only your stomach but also your heart and soul. It's an incredible way to make new friends, learn about different cultures, and create memories that will last forever. So, dear readers, let's embrace the power of food to bring us together and create our own memorable college culinary adventures!

Ready to embark on this delicious journey of social cooking? Let's roll up our sleeves, gather our buddies, and prepare to cook, laugh, sing, and share the love – one tasty bite at a time.

HOSTING POTLUCKS AND THEMED DINNERS

A table heaped with a variety of foods, each lovingly prepared by your friends, has a special way of bringing out the best in everyone. So let's explore the world of potlucks and themed meals. Go grab your apron, and let's dive in!

Potlucks are fantastic because they take the pressure off the host and allow everyone to contribute something special to the meal. Plus, discovering the unique dishes your friends whip up is always a culinary adventure! Let's not forget that the key to a successful potluck is communication. Make sure everyone knows what they're bringing, so you don't end up with seven trays of lasagna (though that doesn't sound too bad, does it?). Also, be mindful of any dietary restrictions, so everyone can enjoy the feast as they deserve.

Now, if you want to kick things up a notch, consider hosting a themed dinner. This can be as simple as "Pizza Night," or you can get creative with themes like "A Trip Around the World" or "Decades Dinner." Themed dinners add a fun twist to your gatherings and inspire your friends to get inventive in the kitchen. Just make sure to plan the menu to have a good range of meals and that everything fits the theme.

To make your potluck or themed dinner even more special, don't forget the ambiance! Set the mood with some fun decorations, create a playlist to match the theme, and maybe even encourage your guests to dress up accordingly. These little but important touches will make your gathering feel extra special and create lasting, beautiful memories. Trust me; your friends will thank you for bringing them together around a table filled with love, laughter, and mouthwatering food.

So, are you ready to embrace the joy of hosting potlucks and themed dinners? Bon appétit, and happy hosting!

PLANNING TIPS

As someone who's been through the college experience and hosted many gatherings, I've got some tried-and-true planning tips to share with you. Just with a little bit of organization and a dash of creativity, you'll create epic events that your friends will be talking about for years to come!

1. Plan ahead

I can't stress this enough! Spontaneous gatherings can be fun, but planning ahead is always the best option when it comes to hosting a larger event or potluck. This gives you and your guests time to prepare and ensures everyone knows what's happening. For instance, I used to send out invites to our legendary "Taco Tuesdays" at least ten days in advance, so everyone could mark their calendars.

2. Delegate tasks

You don't have to do everything by yourself! Task distribution among your friends reduces stress and fosters a sense of responsibility and camaraderie during the planning phase. We'd designate roles like "DJ," "Bartender," or "Decorations Guru" in college to spread out the workload.

3. Choose a theme or menu

Having a theme or specific menu in mind makes planning way easier. For example, we once hosted a "Breakfast for Dinner" potluck, where everyone brought their favorite breakfast meal. Not only was it a blast, but it also made it simple for everyone to decide what to bring.

4. Communicate with your guests

Keep everyone in the loop! Address dietary restrictions, keep guests updated on any changes, and remind everyone about the event a day or two ahead of time. We used to gather two days before each event to brainstorm ideas, ask questions, and get pumped together.

5. Be flexible

Let's face it; things don't always go as planned, and that's okay! Embrace the unexpected and adapt as needed. I remember one time when we planned an outdoor BBQ, and it started pouring rain. Instead of canceling the whole thing, we quickly moved everything indoors and turned it into a memorable and cozy indoor picnic.

6. Enjoy the moment

This is the most important tip of all! Remember that the goal is to create memories, bond with friends, and enjoy the tasty food. So, don't sweat the small stuff and focus on having a good time together.

With these event planning tips and a little practice, you'll be a master event planner in no time. Remember that the most memorable events are those that are filled with laughter, love, and positive energy.

Recipe Suggestions

The key to a successful gathering is having various dishes catering to different tastes and dietary restrictions. So, let's explore some delicious recipes and cooking techniques that were a hit during my college days and always will be!

One-pot wonders

Chili, curry, and pasta dishes that can be made in a single pot are always a hit at potlucks. They are not only convenient to transport, but they also require little cleanup. Mike, a college roommate, used to create a veggie-packed chili that was perfect for both meat-eaters and vegetarians.

Finger foods

Bite-sized snacks like sliders, bruschetta, or spring rolls are ideal for potlucks because they're easy to eat and share. I remember a friend making these incredible Caprese skewers with cherry tomatoes, fresh basil, and mozzarella. And guess what? They were always the first to disappear!

DIY stations

Setting up a DIY station, such as a taco bar, baked potato bar, or build-your-own pizza, allows guests to customize and get creative with their own dishes. My friend Sarah used to host the coolest "Make-Your-Own Sushi" nights, and we all had a great time learning how to create our own sushi rolls with several fillings.

Slow cooker sensations

Slow-cooking foods like pulled pork, meatballs, or mac and cheese can save you time and work while offering exquisite results. My roommate once cooked a fantastic slow-cooker spinach and artichoke dip that had us all coming back for seconds (and thirds).

Crowd-pleasing salads

A big, colorful salad is especially welcome at a potluck or themed dinner. Try a novel dish such as quinoa salad with roasted vegetables or a substantial kale salad with nuts and dried cranberries. One of my friends had a talent for making Instagram-worthy salads that tasted just as amazing as they looked.

Dessert delights

Don't forget about the sweets! Brownies, cookies, and fruit-based desserts are always favorites. A baker friend of mine used to make these amazing lemon bars with the perfect blend of sweet and sour.

<u>Share the love with potlucks</u>

You can encourage your guests to bring their favorite dishes to share. This not only relieves you of the burden of hosting, but it's also a great way to try out new foods and cuisines. We once had an international potluck with everyone bringing a dish from their home country or favorite cuisine, and it was a true culinary journey!

ALLERGEN AND DIETARY RESTRICTIONS CONSIDERATIONS

Let's talk about a key part of planning any gathering: allergens and dietary restrictions. Taking these into consideration can make a huge difference in making everyone feel welcome and included. After all, we want everyone to enjoy the delicious food and have a wonderful time, right? Let me share a few examples from my college days of how we ensured that all of our friends felt included and accepted.

- Communication is key: First and foremost, always ask about any allergies or dietary restrictions your guests may have. We used to include a line in our invites asking for this information, or we'd follow up by ourselves. This allowed us to design the menu accordingly and guarantee that everyone had something to eat.

- Label dishes: Labeling dishes with ingredients and allergens can be a lifesaver when hosting a potluck or buffet-style meal. My roommate, who had a serious allergy to peanuts, was always appreciative when we labeled dishes so she knew exactly what she was able to eat.

- Offer alternatives: Be mindful of providing food options for those with dietary restrictions. We had a vegan friend, so we always made vegan-friendly dishes available at our parties. This not only made her feel included, but it also introduced some tasty plant-based recipes to our non-vegan buddies!

- Educate yourself: Learn the fundamentals of common dietary restrictions such as gluten-free, vegetarian, or lactose-free diets. This will help you plan better and accommodate your guests' needs. We once threw a surprise birthday party for a friend with Celiac disease, and we made sure all the food were gluten-free so she could enjoy herself without any concerns.

- Be mindful of cross-contamination: If you're cooking for someone with food allergies, take extra precautions to avoid cross-contamination. This could imply using separate cutting boards or utensils, or preparing their dish first. I remember that we had a friend who was allergic to shellfish, so we used to cook her portion of pasta separately before adding shrimp to the rest of the dish.

By considering these allergen and dietary restrictions, you'll create a welcoming and inclusive atmosphere for all your guests. In addition, you'll probably end up finding about some new tasty recipes along the way! So, let's raise a toast to being thoughtful hosts and making everyone feel at home.

GROUP-FRIENDLY RECIPES

Let's talk about one of the greatest things ever: group-friendly recipes. You know, those exquisite foods are ideal for sharing with friends and family at get-to-gethers, potlucks, or just a cozy night in with your besties. There's something so magical about gathering around a table filled with food, laughter, love , and good vibes.

One of the best things about group-friendly dishes is that they bring people together in a fun and engaging way. Imagine whipping up a big batch of ho-memade pizzas, with everyone picking their go-to toppings and creating their dream pie. Or how about a sizzling taco night with different tasty fillings, salsas, and toppings for everyone to mix and match? These experiences not only feed our appetites but also create memories that we will cherish for the rest of our lives.

Don't worry if you're not a pro in the kitchen. The good thing about group-frien-dly recipes is that they can be as simple or as elaborate as you like. For example, a big pot of chili or a heaping platter of spaghetti and meatballs may be just as satisfying and delectable as more sophisticated dishes like sushi rolls or tapas.

The key to a successful group-friendly meal is to consider your guests' prefe-rences and dietary restrictions. Make sure that there's something for everyone, from the carnivores to the vegans and the gluten-free folks to the spice lovers. This caring approach will guarantee that everyone feels accepted, included, and fed.

So, what are you waiting for? Go gather your buddies because we are about to explore the delightful realm of group-friendly recipes together. It's a great opportunity to bond, learn new skills, and try new foods while creating special memories that stay with you for the rest of your lives. And hey, who knows? You could just discover your new favorite dish along the way. Happy cooking, then!

PIZZA

Note: Nutrition information may vary
depending on the type of pizza crust used.

CLASSIC MARGHERITA WITH A TWIST

 PREP TIME: 15 MINUTES   **SERVINGS: 4**   **COOKING TIME: 10-12 MINUTES**

INGREDIENTS:

- 1 pre-made pizza crust
- 1/2 cup marinara sauce
- 1/2 teaspoon garlic powder
- 1/2 teaspoon dried oregano
- 1/2 teaspoon dried basil
- 1/4 teaspoon red pepper flakes
- 2 cups shredded mozzarella cheese
- 1 cup cherry tomatoes, halved
- 1/4 cup chopped fresh basil
- 1/4 cup balsamic glaze

DIRECTIONS:

1. Preheat oven to 425°F (220°C).
2. Spread marinara sauce evenly over the pre-made pizza crust.
3. Sprinkle garlic powder, dried oregano, dried basil, and red pepper flakes over the marinara sauce.
4. Sprinkle shredded mozzarella cheese over the top.
5. Top with cherry tomatoes.
6. Bake for 10-12 minutes, or until the cheese is melted and bubbly and the crust is golden brown.
7. Remove from oven and sprinkle with chopped fresh basil.
8. Drizzle balsamic glaze over the top, then slice and serve hot.

Nutritional values: Calories: 246, Total Fat: 10g, Saturated Fat: 6g, Cholesterol: 31mg, Sodium: 578mg, Total Carbohydrates: 26g, Dietary Fiber: 1g, Sugar: 12g, Protein: 14g

BBQ CHICKEN AND VEGGIE DELIGHT

 PREP TIME: 15 MINUTES   **SERVINGS: 4**   **COOK TIME: 15-20 MINUTES**

INGREDIENTS:

- 1 pre-made pizza crust
- 1/2 cup BBQ sauce
- 1 boneless, skinless chicken breast, cooked and shredded
- 1/2 red onion, thinly sliced
- 1/2 green bell pepper, thinly sliced
- 1/2 red bell pepper, thinly sliced
- 1/2 cup canned pineapple chunks, drained
- 2 cups shredded mozzarella cheese

DIRECTIONS:

1. Preheat oven to 425°F (220°C).
2. Spread BBQ sauce evenly over the pre-made pizza crust.
3. Top with shredded chicken, sliced red onion, green and red bell peppers, and pineapple chunks.
4. Sprinkle shredded mozzarella cheese over the top.
5. Bake for 15-20 minutes, or until the cheese is melted and bubbly and the crust is golden brown.
6. Slice and serve hot.

Nutritional values: Calories: 390, Total Fat: 13g, Saturated Fat: 7g, Cholesterol: 54mg, Sodium: 1016mg, Total Carbohydrates: 40g, Dietary Fiber: 3g, Sugar: 18g, Protein: 28g

SPICY PEPPERONI AND JALAPEÑO FIESTA

 PREP TIME: 15 MINUTES　　 **SERVINGS: 8 SLICES**　　 **COOK TIME: 15 MINUTES**

INGREDIENTS:

- 1 pre-made pizza dough (about 16 ounces)
- 1/2 cup marinara or pizza sauce
- 1 1/2 cups shredded mozzarella cheese
- 1/2 cup sliced pepperoni
- 1/4 cup sliced jalapeños (pickled or fresh)
- 1/4 cup sliced red onion
- 1/4 teaspoon crushed red pepper flakes (optional)
- 1/4 teaspoon dried oregano
- 1 tablespoon olive oil
- Cornmeal or flour for dusting

DIRECTIONS:

1. Preheat your oven to 475°F (245°C). If using a pizza stone, place it in the oven to preheat as well. Alternatively, you can use a large baking sheet.
2. On a clean surface dusted with cornmeal or flour, roll out the pizza dough into a 12-14 inch circle or your desired thickness.
3. Carefully transfer the rolled-out dough to the preheated pizza stone or prepared baking sheet.
4. Spread the marinara or pizza sauce evenly over the dough, leaving a small border around the edges.
5. Sprinkle the shredded mozzarella cheese over the sauce, followed by the sliced pepperoni, jalapeños, and red onion.
6. If you like it extra spicy, sprinkle the crushed red pepper flakes over the toppings. Then, add the dried oregano for an extra burst of flavor.
7. Drizzle the olive oil over the pizza and transfer it to the oven.
8. Bake for 12-15 minutes, or until the crust is golden brown and the cheese is melted and bubbly.
9. Remove the pizza from the oven and let it cool for a couple of minutes. Then, slice it into 8 equal pieces and serve immediately.

Nutritional values: Calories: 280 kcal, Protein: 12 g, Carbohydrates: 33 g, Fiber: 2 g, Fat: 11 g, Saturated Fat: 4 g, Cholesterol: 20 mg, Sodium: 620 mg, Potassium: 130 mg, Sugar: 3 g

MEDITERRANEAN MEDLEY WITH FETA AND OLIVES

 PREP TIME: 15 MINUTES   **SERVINGS: 4**   **COOK TIME: 10-12 MINUTES**

INGREDIENTS:

- 1 pre-made pizza crust
- 1/4 cup olive oil
- 1/4 teaspoon garlic powder
- 1/4 teaspoon dried oregano
- 1/4 teaspoon dried basil
- Salt and pepper, to taste
- 2 cups shredded mozzarella cheese
- 1/2 cup crumbled feta cheese
- 1/4 cup sliced Kalamata olives
- 1/4 cup sliced sun-dried tomatoes
- 1/4 cup chopped fresh parsley

DIRECTIONS:

1. Preheat oven to 425°F (220°C).
2. Whisk together the olive oil, garlic powder, dried oregano, dried basil, salt, and pepper in a small bowl.
3. Brush the olive oil mixture evenly over the pre-made pizza crust.
4. Scatter shredded mozzarella cheese over the top.
5. Top with crumbled feta cheese sliced Kalamata olives, and sun-dried tomatoes.
6. Bake for 10-12 minutes, or until the cheese is melted and bubbly and the crust is golden brown.
7. Remove from oven and sprinkle with chopped fresh parsley. Slice and serve hot.

Nutritional values: Calories: 334, Total Fat: 23g, Saturated Fat: 9g, Cholesterol: 44mg, Sodium: 741mg, Total Carbohydrates: 14g, Dietary Fiber: 1g, Sugar: 1g, Protein: 17g

VEGAN PESTO AND ROASTED VEGGIE EXTRAVAGANZA

 PREP TIME: 20 MINUTES   **SERVINGS: 8 SLICES**   **COOK TIME: 25 MINUTES**

INGREDIENTS:

- 1 lb pre-made whole wheat pizza dough
- 1/2 cup vegan basil pesto
- 1 cup thinly sliced zucchini
- 1 cup thinly sliced bell peppers (mixed colors)
- 1 cup halved cherry tomatoes
- 1/2 cup thinly sliced red onion
- 1/2 cup sliced Kalamata olives
- 1/4 cup chopped fresh basil
- 1 tablespoon olive oil
- Salt and pepper to taste
- 1 cup shredded vegan mozzarella cheese (optional)

DIRECTIONS:

1. Preheat your oven to 450°F (230°C). If you're using a pizza stone, place it in the oven to preheat.
2. On a lightly floured surface, roll out the pizza dough into a 12-inch circle or a rectangle, depending on your preference.
3. In a large mixing bowl, toss the zucchini, bell peppers, cherry tomatoes, red onion, and Kalamata olives with olive oil, salt, and pepper.
4. Carefully transfer the rolled-out dough onto the preheated stone if using a pizza stone. If not, place the dough on a parchment-lined baking sheet.
5. Spread the vegan basil pesto evenly over the pizza dough, leaving a small border around the edges.
6. Arrange the seasoned vegetables on top of the pesto, and sprinkle with vegan mozzarella cheese if desired.
7. Bake the pizza in the oven for 20-25 minutes or until the crust is golden brown and the vegetables are tender.
8. Remove the pizza from the oven and allow it to cool for a few minutes before garnishing it with fresh basil.
9. Slice the pizza into eight pieces and serve immediately.

Nutritional values: Calories: 290 kcal, Protein: 7 g, Carbohydrates: 44 g, Fiber: 6 g, Fat: 11 g, Saturated Fat: 1.5 g, Sodium: 560 mg, Potassium: 210 mg, Sugar: 4 g

HAWAIIAN DELIGHT

 PREP TIME: 15 MINUTES   **SERVINGS: 4**   **COOK TIME: 10-12 MINUTES**

INGREDIENTS:

- 1 pre-made pizza crust
- 1/2 cup pizza sauce
- 1/2 teaspoon garlic powder
- 1/2 teaspoon dried oregano
- 1/2 teaspoon dried basil
- 2 cups shredded mozzarella cheese
- 1/2 cup diced ham
- 1/2 cup diced pineapple

DIRECTIONS:

1. Preheat oven to 425°F (220°C).
2. Spread pizza sauce evenly over the pre-made pizza crust.
3. Sprinkle garlic powder, dried oregano, and dried basil over the pizza sauce.
4. Sprinkle shredded mozzarella cheese over the top. Top with diced ham and diced pineapple.
5. Bake for 10-12 minutes, or until the cheese is melted and bubbly and the crust is golden brown.
6. Slice and serve hot.

Nutritional values: Calories: 308, Total Fat: 17g, Saturated Fat: 8g, Cholesterol: 50mg, Sodium: 798mg, Total Carbohydrates: 20g, Dietary Fiber: 1g, Sugar: 8g, Protein: 19g

TACOS AND FAJITAS

Note: Nutrition facts may vary depending on the toppings you choose to add.

SPICY CHIPOTLE CHICKEN TACOS

 PREP TIME: 15 MINUTES   **SERVINGS: 4**

INGREDIENTS:

- 1 lb. boneless, skinless chicken breast, cut into small pieces
- 1 tbsp. olive oil
- Salt and pepper, to taste
- 1/2 cup diced onion
- 1/2 cup chopped bell pepper (any color)
- 2 cloves garlic, minced
- 1-2 chipotle peppers in adobo sauce, minced
- 1 tsp. chili powder
- 1/2 tsp. ground cumin
- 1/4 tsp. paprika
- 1/4 tsp. dried oregano
- 1/4 tsp. garlic powder
- 1/4 tsp. onion powder
- 1/4 tsp. salt
- 1/4 cup chicken broth
- 8-10 small tortillas, warmed
- Optional toppings: shredded lettuce, diced tomatoes, shredded cheese, cilantro, avocado, salsa, sour cream, lime wedges

DIRECTIONS:

1. Heat the olive oil in a large skillet over medium-high heat. Add the diced chicken to the pan and season with salt and pepper. Cook the chicken for 5-7 minutes or until browned and cooked through. Remove the chicken from the pan and set it aside on a plate.

2. In the same skillet, add the diced onion and bell pepper. Cook for 3-4 minutes or until the vegetables are slightly softened. Add the minced garlic and chipotle peppers to the pan, and cook for an additional 1-2 minutes.

3. Add the chili powder, cumin, paprika, oregano, garlic powder, onion powder, and salt to the pan. Stir well to combine the spices with the vegetables.

4. Pour the chicken broth into the skillet and stir to combine. Add the cooked chicken back to the pan and stir to coat it in the spicy sauce. Cook for 2-3 minutes or until the sauce has thickened slightly.

5. Serve the spicy chipotle chicken in warm tortillas, and top with your favorite toppings. Enjoy!

Nutritional values: Calories: 392, Fat: 11g, Saturated Fat: 2g, Cholesterol: 83mg, Sodium: 700mg, Carbohydrates: 38g, Fiber: 5g, Sugar: 4g, Protein: 35g

VEGGIE-PACKED BLACK BEAN FAJITAS

 PREP TIME: 15 MINUTES    **SERVINGS: 4**

INGREDIENTS:

- 2 tbsp. olive oil
- 1 red onion, sliced
- 1 red bell pepper, sliced
- 1 yellow bell pepper, sliced
- 1 green bell pepper, sliced
- 1 zucchini, sliced
- 1 yellow squash, sliced
- 3 cloves garlic, minced
- 1 tbsp. chili powder
- 1 tsp. ground cumin
- 1 tsp. smoked paprika
- 1/2 tsp. dried oregano
- 1/2 tsp. salt
- 1/4 tsp. black pepper
- 1 can black beans, drained and rinsed
- 8-10 small tortillas, warmed
- **Optional toppings:** shredded lettuce, diced tomatoes, shredded cheese, cilantro, avocado, salsa, sour cream, lime wedges

DIRECTIONS:

1. Heat the olive oil in a large skillet over medium-high heat. Add the sliced onion and bell peppers to the pan, and cook for 5-7 minutes until the vegetables are slightly softened.
2. Add the sliced zucchini and yellow squash to the pan, and cook for 3-4 minutes or until the vegetables are tender.
3. Add the minced garlic, chili powder, cumin, smoked paprika, oregano, salt, and black pepper to the pan. Stir well to combine the spices with the vegetables.
4. Add the black beans to the pan, and stir to combine. Cook for an additional 2-3 minutes or until the beans are heated through.
5. Serve the veggie-packed black bean mixture in warm tortillas and top with your favorite toppings. Enjoy!

Note: You can customize the recipe by adding or substituting different veggies based on your preferences. You can also use a store-bought fajita seasoning mix instead of the individual spices listed in the recipe.

Nutritional values: Calories: 320, Fat: 10g, Saturated Fat: 1g, Cholesterol: 0mg, Sodium: 680mg, Carbohydrates: 51g, Fiber: 15g, Sugar: 8g, Protein: 13g

GRILLED SHRIMP TACOS WITH AVOCADO SALSA

 PREP TIME: 20 MINUTES   **SERVINGS: 4**

INGREDIENTS:

- 1 lb. large shrimp, peeled and deveined
- 1 tbsp. olive oil
- 1 tsp. chili powder
- 1/2 tsp. ground cumin
- 1/2 tsp. garlic powder
- 1/4 tsp. salt
- 1/4 tsp. black pepper
- 8-10 small tortillas, warmed
- **Optional toppings:** shredded lettuce, diced tomatoes, shredded cheese, cilantro, lime wedges

For the Avocado Salsa:

- 2 ripe avocados, diced
- 1/2 red onion, diced
- 1 small jalapeno, seeded and minced
- 1/4 cup chopped fresh cilantro
- Juice of 1 lime
- Salt and pepper, to taste

DIRECTIONS:

1. Preheat a grill or grill pan to medium-high heat.
2. Whisk together the olive oil, chili powder, cumin, garlic powder, salt, and black pepper in a small bowl. Add the shrimp to the bowl and toss to coat.
3. Grill the shrimp for 2-3 minutes per side or until they are pink and slightly charred.
4. While the shrimp is cooking, prepare the avocado salsa. Combine the diced avocados, red onion, jalapeno, cilantro, lime juice, salt, and pepper in a medium bowl. Stir well to combine.
5. To assemble the tacos, place a few shrimp on a warm tortilla, and top it with a spoonful of avocado salsa. You can add additional toppings, such as shredded lettuce or diced tomatoes. Repeat with the remaining tortillas and filling.
6. Serve the tacos with lime wedges on the side.

Nutritional values: Calories: 405, Fat: 20g, Saturated Fat: 3g, Cholesterol: 172mg, Sodium: 521mg, Carbohydrates: 35g, Fiber: 10g, Sugar: 3g, Protein: 25g

SLOW COOKER CARNITAS TACOS

 PREP TIME: 15 MINUTES    **SERVINGS: 6**    **COOK TIME: 8 HOURS**

INGREDIENTS:

- 3 lbs. boneless pork shoulder, trimmed and cut into 2-inch pieces
- 1 tbsp. olive oil
- 1 tsp. salt
- 1/2 tsp. black pepper
- 2 tsp. chili powder
- 1 tsp. ground cumin
- 1 tsp. smoked paprika
- 1/2 tsp. garlic powder
- 1/2 tsp. onion powder
- 1/2 tsp. dried oregano
- 1/2 cup orange juice
- 1/4 cup lime juice
- 1 onion, chopped
- 4 cloves garlic, minced
- 12-16 small tortillas, warmed
- **Optional toppings:** diced tomatoes, shredded cheese, chopped cilantro, lime wedges

DIRECTIONS:

1. Whisk together the salt, black pepper, chili powder, cumin, smoked paprika, garlic powder, onion powder, and oregano in a small bowl.

2. Place the trimmed pork shoulder pieces in a slow cooker. Drizzle the olive oil over the pork, and sprinkle the spice mixture. Use your hands to rub the spices into the pork, ensuring all the pieces are coated.

3. Add the slow cooker's orange juice, lime juice, chopped onion, and minced garlic. Stir well to combine.

4. Cover the slow cooker and cook on low for 8 hours or until the pork is tender and easily shreds with a fork.

5. Remove the pork from the slow cooker and shred it with two forks. Return the shredded pork to the slow cooker and stir it into the juices and onions.

6. Place spoonfuls of the carnitas to assemble the tacos on a warm tortilla. Top with any additional toppings you like, such as diced tomatoes, shredded cheese, or chopped cilantro. Repeat with the remaining tortillas and filling.

7. Serve the tacos with lime wedges on the side.

Nutritional values: Calories: 377, Fat: 18g, Saturated Fat: 6g, Cholesterol: 136mg, Sodium: 727mg, Carbohydrates: 23g, Fiber: 3g, Sugar: 3g, Protein: 30g

SMOKY TOFU FAJITAS WITH PEPPERS AND ONIONS

 PREP TIME: 5 MINUTES   **SERVINGS: 4**    **COOK TIME: 15 MINUTES**

INGREDIENTS:

- 1 block of extra-firm tofu, drained and pressed
- 1 red bell pepper, sliced
- 1 yellow bell pepper, sliced
- 1 green bell pepper, sliced
- 1 red onion, sliced
- 2 tbsp. olive oil
- 1 tsp. chili powder
- 1 tsp. smoked paprika
- 1/2 tsp. garlic powder
- 1/2 tsp. onion powder
- 1/2 tsp. cumin
- 1/2 tsp. salt
- 1/4 tsp. black pepper
- 8-10 small tortillas, warmed
- **Optional toppings:** shredded lettuce, diced tomatoes, shredded cheese, cilantro, lime wedges

DIRECTIONS:

1. Preheat the oven to 400°F. Line a baking sheet with parchment paper.
2. Cut the tofu into strips or cubes.
3. Whisk together the chili powder, smoked paprika, garlic powder, onion powder, cumin, salt, and black pepper in a small bowl. Sprinkle the spice mixture over the tofu and toss to coat.
4. Spread the tofu on the prepared baking sheet and bake for 15-20 minutes or until the tofu is slightly crispy and browned.
5. While the tofu is cooking, heat the olive oil in a large skillet over medium-high heat. Add the sliced peppers and onions to the skillet and cook for 5 minutes or until the vegetables are slightly softened.
6. Add the cooked tofu to the skillet with the peppers and onions. Stir well to combine and heat through.
7. Place a few spoonfuls of the tofu and pepper mixture on a warm tortilla to assemble the fajitas. Repeat with the remaining tortillas and filling. Top with any additional toppings you like, such as shredded lettuce, diced tomatoes, or shredded cheese.
8. Serve the fajitas with lime wedges on the side, and enjoy.

Nutritional values: Calories: 300, Fat: 13g, Saturated Fat: 2g, Cholesterol: 0mg, Sodium: 540mg, Carbohydrates: 32g, Fiber: 6g, Sugar: 5g, Protein: 14g

DIY SUSHI ROLLS

CRISPY TEMPURA VEGGIE ROLL

 PREP TIME: 30 MINUTES    **SERVINGS: 4 ROLLS (24-32 PIECES)**   **COOK TIME: 15 MINUTES**

INGREDIENTS:

- 4 sheets nori (seaweed)
- 2 cups sushi rice, cooked and seasoned
- 1 cup tempura batter mix
- 1 cup cold water
- 1 medium zucchini, cut into thin strips
- 1 medium sweet potato, cut into thin strips
- 1 small bell pepper, cut into thin strips
- 1 medium carrot, cut into thin strips
- Vegetable oil for frying
- Soy sauce for dipping
- **Optional:** wasabi and pickled ginger

DIRECTIONS:

1. In a deep frying pan or pot, heat vegetable oil to 375°F (190°C) for deep-frying.
2. In a mixing bowl, combine the tempura batter mix and cold water, whisking until smooth.
3. Dip the zucchini, sweet potato, bell pepper, and carrot strips into the tempura batter, ensuring they're fully coated.
4. Carefully place the battered vegetables into the hot oil, frying them for 2-3 minutes or until they're crispy and golden brown. Use a slotted spoon to transfer the fried veggies to a paper towel-lined plate to drain excess oil.
5. Place a sheet of nori, shiny side down, on a bamboo sushi mat. Spread about 1/2 cup of sushi rice evenly over the nori, leaving a 1-inch (2.5 cm) border at the top.
6. Arrange a few pieces of the crispy tempura veggies along the bottom edge of the rice-covered nori.
7. Using the bamboo mat, roll the sushi tightly, applying gentle pressure as you go. Seal the roll by moistening the exposed nori edge with water. Repeat with the remaining ingredients to make four rolls in total.
8. Use a sharp knife to slice each sushi roll into 6-8 pieces. Serve with soy sauce for dipping, optional wasabi, and pickled ginger on the side.

Nutritional values: Calories: 480 kcal, Protein: 10 g, Carbohydrates: 90 g, Fiber: 4 g, Fat: 10 g, Saturated Fat: 1 g, Sodium: 400 mg, Potassium: 450 mg, Sugar: 5 g

SPICY TUNA CRUNCH ROLL

 PREP TIME: 20 MINUTES    **SERVINGS: 4-6**

INGREDIENTS:

- 2 cups sushi rice
- 2 cups water
- 1/4 cup rice vinegar
- 2 tbsp. sugar
- 1 tsp. salt
- 4-6 sheets of sushi nori
- 1/2 lb. sushi-grade tuna, diced
- 2 tbsp. mayonnaise
- 1-2 tsp. sriracha, to taste
- 1/2 cup panko breadcrumbs
- 1 tbsp. vegetable oil
- **Optional toppings:** sesame seeds, sliced avocado, sliced cucumber, soy sauce, wasabi

DIRECTIONS:

1. Rinse the sushi rice in a fine-mesh strainer until the water runs clear. Combine the rinsed rice and 2 cups of water in a medium saucepan. Bring to a boil, reduce the heat to low and cover the pan. Cook until the rice is tender and the water has been absorbed (18-20 minutes).

2. While the rice is cooking, combine the rice vinegar, sugar, and salt in a small saucepan. Heat over low heat until the sugar and salt have dissolved. Set aside to cool.

3. When the rice is done cooking, transfer it to a large bowl. Add the cooled vinegar mixture to the rice and stir well to combine. Allow the rice to cool to room temperature.

4. In a small bowl, combine the diced tuna, mayonnaise, and sriracha. Stir well to combine.

5. In a small skillet, heat the vegetable oil over medium heat. Add the panko breadcrumbs and cook, frequently stirring, until golden brown and crispy.

6. To assemble the rolls, place a sheet of sushi nori on a sushi mat or a piece of plastic wrap. Spread a thin layer of the sushi rice over the nori, leaving a 1-inch border at the top.

7. Spoon the tuna mixture over the rice, spreading it in an even layer. Sprinkle the crispy panko breadcrumbs over the tuna.

8. Using the sushi mat or plastic wrap, roll the sushi tightly into a cylinder. Wet the border with a little bit of water to help it seal.

9. Repeat with the remaining nori sheets and fillings.

10. Use a sharp knife to slice the rolls into 1-inch pieces. Serve with optional toppings such as sesame seeds, sliced avocado, sliced cucumber, soy sauce, or wasabi.

Nutritional values: Calories: 360, Fat: 10g, Saturated Fat: 2g, Cholesterol: 35mg, Sodium: 550mg, Carbohydrates: 51g, Fiber: 2g, Sugar: 5g, Protein: 16g

CALIFORNIA DREAM ROLL

 PREP TIME: 25 MINUTES

 **SERVINGS: 4 ROLLS (32 PIECES)**

INGREDIENTS:

- 4 nori seaweed sheets
- 2 cups cooked sushi rice (short-grain rice mixed with rice vinegar, sugar, and salt)
- 1 avocado, sliced
- 1 cucumber, seeded and julienned
- 1/2 pound cooked crabmeat or imitation crab
- 2 tablespoons sesame seeds (optional)
- Soy sauce for serving
- Pickled ginger for serving
- Wasabi, for serving

DIRECTIONS:

1. Place a sheet of nori on a bamboo sushi mat, shiny side down. Wet your hands with water to prevent sticking, then spread approximately 1/2 cup of sushi rice evenly over the nori, leaving a 1-inch margin at the top edge.

2. Lay a row of avocado slices, cucumber sticks, and crabmeat (or imitation crab) horizontally across the center of the rice-covered nori.

3. Roll the sushi away from you, tucking the fillings tightly and applying gentle pressure to the roll. Gently grip the edge of the bamboo mat closest to you with your thumbs while holding the fillings in place with your fingers. Use the bamboo mat to shape and compress the roll.

4. Cut the roll into 8 equal pieces using a sharp, wet knife. If desired, sprinkle the rolls with sesame seeds for extra flavor and texture.

5. Repeat steps 1-4 with the remaining ingredients to make four rolls.

6. Serve the California Dream Rolls with soy sauce, pickled ginger, and wasabi on the side.

Nutritional values: Calories: 330 kcal, Protein: 12 g, Carbohydrates: 52 g, Fiber: 5 g, Fat: 9 g, Saturated Fat: 1 g, Cholesterol: 20 mg (if using real crab meat), Sodium: 550 mg, Potassium: 420 mg, Sugar: 4 g

TERIYAKI CHICKEN AND AVOCADO ROLL

 PREP TIME: 30 MINUTES   **SERVINGS: 4 ROLLS**

INGREDIENTS:

- 4 Nori sheets
- 2 cups sushi rice, cooked
- 1 avocado, sliced
- 1 chicken breast, cooked and shredded
- 1/4 cup teriyaki sauce
- 1/2 cucumber, julienned
- 1 tsp sesame seeds

DIRECTIONS:

1. Lay a Nori sheet on a sushi mat, shiny side down.
2. Spread a thin layer of cooked sushi rice on the Nori sheet, leaving a small border on the top edge.
3. Arrange the avocado, shredded chicken, and cucumber in a line across the center of the rice.
4. Drizzle teriyaki sauce over the chicken.
5. Sprinkle sesame seeds over the top.
6. Roll up the Nori sheet tightly using the sushi mat, pressing down gently.
7. Repeat with the remaining Nori sheets and ingredients.
8. Slice each roll into eight pieces and serve.

Nutritional values: Calories: 250, Fat: 7g, Saturated Fat: 1.5g, Cholesterol: 30mg, Sodium: 450mg, Carbohydrates: 35g, Fiber: 4g, Sugar: 6g, Protein: 10g

SMOKED SALMON AND CREAM CHEESE ROLL

 PREP TIME: 30 MINUTES   **SERVINGS: 4 ROLLS**

INGREDIENTS:

- 4 Nori sheets
- 2 cups sushi rice, cooked
- 4 oz smoked salmon, sliced
- 4 oz cream cheese, softened
- 1/2 cucumber, julienned
- 1 tsp sesame seeds

DIRECTIONS:

1. Lay a Nori sheet on a sushi mat, shiny side down.
2. Spread a thin layer of cooked sushi rice on the Nori sheet, leaving a small border on the top edge.
3. Spread a thin layer of cream cheese over the rice.
4. Arrange the smoked salmon and cucumber in a line across the center of the rice.
5. Sprinkle sesame seeds over the top.
6. Roll up the Nori sheet tightly using the sushi mat, pressing down gently.
7. Repeat with the remaining Nori sheets and ingredients.
8. Slice each roll into eight pieces and serve.

Nutritional values: Calories: 280, Fat: 15g, Saturated Fat: 8g, Cholesterol: 50mg, Sodium: 400mg, Carbohydrates: 25g, Fiber: 2g, Sugar: 2g, Protein: 12g

CONCLUSION

Congratulations, you made it to the end of the cookbook! By now, I'm sure that you feel more confident and excited about cooking in the kitchen. Remember that cooking is more than just preparing a meal; it's also about the experience, creativity, and fun that comes with it.

Throughout this book, we've explored many recipes ranging from quick meals to more sophisticated dishes. You have learned new tips and tricks to help you explore your cooking skills and become a better cook. Don't shy away from experimenting, and make changes to the recipes to fit your taste and preferences.

Overall, I'm all about cooking at home because it has countless advantages to it! It saves you lots of money and allows you to control what goes into your food. You can make better and healthier choices and cook meals that fit your dietary needs. Cooking is also a great way to bond with friends and family, or even impress a date!

Before you leave, let me share a quick story that I'm sure will leave you feeling inspired.

My first year of college was spent in a small dorm room with an ancient mini-fridge and a microwave. Like many other students, I relied heavily on fast food and ready-made meals. But, one day I came up with a simple recipe for baked ziti online and decided to give it a try.

And surprisingly, the ziti turned out yummy, and I felt a sense of pride and accomplishment I had never experienced in my entire life. In fact, I really liked the idea of experimenting with ingredients and started to explore my cooking skills with more recipes, using whatever ingredients I had on hand.

And before I knew it, I was cooking delicious meals for my roommates, and we would gather in our tiny dorm room to enjoy homemade meals together. And guess what? My meals got lots of compliments! There, I realized how much I loved food and how cooking brought people together. That experience totally inspired me and sparked my passion for cooking, and I eventually decided to pursue it as a career. Now, many years later, I'm grateful for that small dorm room and the unforgettable memories it holds.

My point is, don't be afraid to experiment. Try new things in the kitchen to see and taste the amazing places and journeys it takes you!

Cooking is a learning process; the more you do it, the better you'll get. So, go ahead and try out the recipes in this book. Remember to have fun, be creative, and don't worry about making mistakes. With over 150 recipes, you'll definitely find something you love.

Thank you for choosing this cookbook, and good luck with your cooking experience!

THANKS!

Thank you for diving into "The No-Fuss College Cookbook" and discovering the world of easy and delicious college cooking! To show our appreciation, we have an exclusive FREE BONUS just for you: "Morning After Mastery: Hangover Recovery Hacks for College Students" – your essential blueprint for bouncing back after a wild night out.

This powerful and practical ebook is packed with tried-and-tested tips, including revitalizing recipes, to help you conquer those dreaded hangover blues. To claim your free bonus, simply scan this QR code:

We hope you've enjoyed the recipes and culinary inspiration in "The No-Fuss College Cookbook". If you've found this cookbook helpful, please take a moment to leave a review on Amazon. Your feedback not only helps future readers but also supports our mission to create more valuable content.

Thank you once again for your support, and happy cooking!

Lydia Merrill

ABOUT THE AUTHOR

Lydia Merrill is a certified Dietician and Nutritionist with over 20 years of experience counseling individuals on sustainable weight management and disease prevention.

She is the best-selling author of several cookbooks and is passionate about coffee. In her years of practice, Merrill has helped countless individuals improve their health and well-being through dietary and lifestyle changes. She is known for her approachable and practical advice and her ability to make healthy eating enjoyable and sustainable.

When she's not working, Merrill can be found experimenting in the kitchen or sipping on her favorite cup of coffee.

Made in the USA
Middletown, DE
24 August 2024

59659261R00117